E. J. Mishan

Twenty-one Popular Economic Fallacies

With an introduction by
Kurt Klappholz

Allen Lane The Penguin Press

Contents

Preface

With the growth in technology over the past 200 years, especially with the growth in transport and communications, control of political power has gravitated towards the centre. During the same period this political power has penetrated more deeply into society. Modern legislation has far-reaching repercussions on every aspect of our private and working lives at a time when the citizen's power to influence the course of political events is remote and limited. Even when account is taken of the greater political effectiveness of organized campaigns and lobbies, the diversity of interests and opinions found in the large populations of highly developed countries goes far to ensure that the resulting legislation will be a compromise that pleases no one and irritates many.* For all that, political aspirations towards greater economic self-sufficiency and greater power in world affairs strengthen the movement towards larger political and geographical units. The resultant dilemma is but one instance of the thesis that the momenta set up by rapid economic growth,

*In an earlier age, when the aspirations of ordinary men and women were modest and their political horizons bounded by their immediate localities, frustrations were fewer. Today, events taking place on the other side of the world are known to us, are indeed seen and heard by us, at the very time they are happening. And it is the devoted task of an army of newsmen and commentators to impress the public with a sense of urgency and involvement in them. Yet if the influence the ordinary citizen can hope to exert on national issues is slight, on international affairs it is all but negligible. In view of the passionate and partisan feelings sometimes aroused by political issues, national and international, over which any one citizen or group exercises little control − if only because their convictions collide with those of other individuals or groups − the occasional recourse to unlawful means of protest, though reprehensible and dangerous, is not altogether surprising.

Preface

on the one hand, and the intuitive wants of ordinary men, on the other, are beginning to pull in opposite directions.* At a time when our political leaders (representing, as they believe, the 'progressive' forces associated with the new technology) are most impatient to integrate Britain with a sovereign Europe, separationist movements are gathering force in Scotland and Wales and finding popular expression in the more general movement for regional decentralization.

Rapid economic growth in the West has, however, contributed to the frustrations of the governed in another way, one arising from the apparent complexity of modern social and economic problems. As a consequence there is a noticeable tendency, in Britain at least, for governments to avoid the irksomeness of justifying their policies to the public except in the most superficial way. Too often this takes the form of assurances that the government has taken 'expert advice' and/or consulted with all groups directly concerned. We are then expected to believe that the particular measures adopted by the government can be depended on to further the 'national interest'.

If the policies governments today seek to implement had only limited impact on our well-being, their impatience to 'get on with the job' would not matter so much. But, as suggested, they affect our lives intimately. Moreover, the magnitude of events taking place today is quite without parallel in history. We live on the brink of ecological disaster, a consequence of the eruption of world population and the heedless spread of the products of chemical technology. The mounting spillover effects of modern industry; the havoc that follows the growth of motorized transport; the new forms of social strife following an unprecedented revolution in communications and, in its wake, a rising tide of unrealizable expectations – such developments have brought us to an era that quakes from day to day with incipient crises, and from which no man may hope to find refuge. In these circumstances, the political decisions taken by the government during its tenure of office can have drastic consequences, for

*A thesis that is elaborated in my *Costs of Economic Growth* (Staples Press, 1967).

8

better or for worse, on the condition of our society. One need
only think of the attempts of two governments to take Britain
into Europe, the legislation put into effect to encourage air
travel over Britain and to promote supersonic flight, and the
decision, until the Act of 1962, to allow unlimited Commonwealth immigration into Britain. Whether the reader approves
of these policies or not, he will surely agree that each of them
bears intimately on the quality of our lives and the character
of our society. He deceives himself, however, if he believes that
in any one of these cases there has been a broadly based and
informed debate on their economic and social consequences.

To some extent, the lack of critical public discussion on such
issues is a result of both government and opposition leaders
being under the influence of the same obsolete 'forward-looking'
liberal ideology. And it is no comfort to know that in these
turbulent days the country is still in the hands of men whose
political responses are habitually guided by the economic
presumptions of a bygone era; men who appear to regard it as
self-evident that any increase in the speed of economic growth,
any rise in the rate of technological innovation, any increase in
the mobility of populations, any expansion of exports or of
gross national product or of adult education can only serve to
bring us the sooner into the millennium. Yet it is just because
these propositions are accepted as axiomatic by so many men in
public life that debate on political issues having the most far-
reaching importance for the British people has been perfunctory
and evasive.

But in part, the lack of informed debate can be blamed on the
professional economist not only for neglecting to provide
the public with a clear understanding of the implications of the
policies being pursued but also for neglecting to inform the
public at all times of the range of alternative economic policies.
Unaided, the public cannot be expected to penetrate the smoke-
screen of economic confusion and mysticism (so ably generated
by ministers and news commentators) behind which the leaders
of both parties pursue their wilful ways.

In the circumstances, reference to expert advice at the disposal of governments is unacceptable. It cannot be emphasized too often that the choice of policy should never be left to the expert. The task of the expert is, as indicated, restricted to that of presenting relevant information either to the public directly or else to the government for the clear purpose of enabling it to initiate informed debate on the question.* Whether a consensus can be reached or not, any defence by the government that its actions are guided by impartial and expert economic counsel is wholly unacceptable – even where the government's economic advisers are highly regarded within the profession. For recourse to expert advice effectively leaves the choice of social ends (which, in the last resort, is the business of the citizen) in the hands of the expert.

It may be surmised in passing, however, that it is unlikely that the government's economic policy is ever guided wholly by impartial and expert economic counsel. At the policy level, British governments are not unknown to consult or to employ economists believed to be sympathetic to their doctrines and to the sort of programmes that seem to emerge from them. Even if the economist, entering the government's employ in a position of authority, has no political preconceptions, he may soon find himself paying homage to those held by the existing establishment. The promptings of ambition, a perfectly natural desire to be of some use to the government, the need to get along with the people about him, politicians and civil servants, all combine to start him thinking about a problem in terms of what is 'politically feasible'. He may believe, for example, that a

---

*A qualification for this view can perhaps be made for a broad range of economic problems which may be resolved by skilled application of certain familiar techniques (for instance, cost–benefit studies) derived from criteria that are themselves based on widely accepted ethical premises.

In the present imperfect state of the subject, however, there can be differences within the profession on what qualify as agenda, on the methods of measurement, and on the construction of the 'model' itself. In order that the public, and other economists in the country, can scrutinize the methods used and the estimates reached, and subject them to informed criticism, the government has an obligation to make public all cost–benefit studies designed to influence its decisions.

floating exchange rate (along with certain safeguards) offers the most promising solution to the perennial balance-of-payments difficulties. But if he learns from experience that 'it is just not on the cards', he can only annoy other people to no purpose by being insistent on bringing it into the debate. Rather than be ignored or resented he will be inclined to accept, 'provisionally' at least, constraints on the range of technically practicable alternatives. Inadvertently then he fails in his duty to the public and finds himself placing the imprimatur of his expertise at the disposal of the government's predilections. The ideal conduct of the expert, that of disclosing as objectively as he can the consequences of the full range of alternative economic policies in the light of the most recent research – not only to the government but to the public at large – cannot be realized in these circumstances. Indeed, the government's economist is likely to find himself fully occupied offering 'technical' advice on implementing the government's programme. All the greater then is the need for the concerned public to be fully informed on economic matters.

One way of achieving this desideratum is that practised today in the United States. Professional economists there – indeed top-flight economists of the academic stature of Milton Friedman, Paul Samuelson and James Tobin – are willing to turn from the study of fascinating arcane matter for the express purpose of clarifying current issues so enabling the intelligent citizen the better to judge and participate in the debate. The prospect is both attractive and feasible, and should be encouraged. Without bandying jargon or exhibiting formulae, without being superficial or condescending, the scientist should be able to communicate to the public the nature and variety of consequences that can reasonably be expected to flow from a given action or sequence of actions. In the case of the economist, he can sometimes do a little more than that. He can often reveal in an informal way, if not the detailed chain of reasoning by which he reaches his conclusions, at least the broad contours of the argument.

An alternative – that pursued here – is to expose the politically conscious citizen to the shock treatment of discovering that much of what passes for economic truism is in fact fallacious. If the former method has the advantage of dealing with the immediate issues in the news, the latter (adopted here) has the advantage of a more leisurely approach. It claims greater 'depth' of treatment, and may appeal to readers who find the task of digesting even the popular writings of professional economists a little exacting. But the two methods are obviously complementary. Both have much to contribute to the habit of informed and articulate scepticism among the populace that is the bane of governments and the lifeblood of democracy.

*

It would be presumptuous to believe that a single volume dedicated to exposing a number of the more persistent fallacies, even if it is received by the public with enthusiasm, will effectively exorcize them from their long sojourn in our society. As Sir Thomas Browne observes in his *Religio Medici*:

Heresies perish not with their Authors but, like the river *Arethusa*, though they lose their currents in one place, they rise up in another. One general Council is not able to extirpate one single Heresie; it may be cancell'd for the present; but revolution of time, and the like aspects from Heaven, will restore it, when it will flourish till it be condemned again.*

This, however, may be too pessimistic a philosophy for an age such as ours, one boasting over-developed media of communication. At all events, the more frequently that false arguments are attacked the smaller the influence they will come to exert. Governments, impatient to push through programmes alleged – inevitably – to be in the public interest, will not be able to depend upon them, as they do now, to quieten opposition in the country. Often enough the sound instinct of individuals or groups will incline them to reject proposed legislation. But because their arguments are deficient in economic essentials, they cannot effectively rebut the government's arguments. Such

*I am indebted for this reference to Dr Lionel Needleman.

considerations may seem to warrant the appearance of the present volume. It may do good. Can it do any harm?

Worse than the blind leading the blind is the deluded leading them. Since it studies a somewhat volatile universe, economics can boast only a limited stock of accepted principles. Well-tested theories are few and often highly qualified: by far the greater part of modern economics lies within the area of speculation and controversy. Consequently, there is plenty of room for differences of opinion between professionals in expounding even the elements of the subject.

It might then be concluded that although these excursions into topical questions will arouse his interest and stimulate his curiosity, the reader who places his credulity at the author's disposal cannot be guaranteed a safe conduct. But in fact the reader's prospects are, or should be, fairly bright. After making full allowance for the wide area of current controversy in economics, a statement that is rightly alleged to be a fallacy should be recognized as a fallacy by the mass of academic economists. For in declaring a statement to be fallacious one is not sticking one's neck out very far. One is not asserting a positive proposition. One is merely repudiating, as being untenable, what others assert to be true. And what is asserted to be true, and what in fact is often widely thought to be true, may easily be shown to be untenable by revealing inadequacies in the argument or in the data. If therefore one can show, for instance, that a popular conclusion about the effects of rising real income is invalid by reference to the ordinary rules of logic and/or those of scientific evidence, one may legitimately hope for general agreement among the profession that the conclusion in question is indeed invalid.

By widely accepted criteria, then, the would-be debunker can be clearly right or wrong. And if it transpires that not all of the statements he alleges to be fallacies are in fact fallacies he must take full responsibility for misleading the reader. In any case, he cannot hope to escape the strictures of the critical reviewer. But it is also important that the existing public complacency about economics be ruffled a little, and that post-war orthodoxies

Preface

– such as the belief that only a faster rate of economic growth can be counted on to overcome inflation or to improve the country's balance of payments – be exposed for the humbug they are. To use the current jargon, the time has come for 'a more meaningful dialogue' about economic issues within society; meaningful enough to impress on the intelligent public that economics is at least as much about *choice* as about *necessity*; and that there is a good deal more to economic sagacity than repeated exhortations for harder work and more sacrifice.

*

In talking of fallacies I use the word in its broader meaning to cover unsound argument as well as false notions about the universe, and I extend it somewhat to cover misconceptions of the issue (as in the discussion of the so-called brain drain and of advertising) and also incomplete appreciation of the complexity of the problem (as in the discussion of the effects of economic union with Europe and of the connection between economic growth and enrichment).

The twenty-one fallacies treated in this volume, however, provide only a small sample from the large number in active circulation. The principle of selection was weighted in favour of those which appeared to be among the most influential in current economic topics. A glance through the table of contents will, I hope, bear this out. But there are several others – those in Part 2 in particular – which a large number of people, certainly a large number of businessmen, would regard as self-evident. These form part of the implicit premisses on which economic policy, often very bad economic policy, is raised. The reader will soon appreciate that a particular concept employed to dissect one fallacious argument may be usefully employed in several other fallacies also. Cross-references will draw his attention to a number of such instances.

I can fairly claim, though without perverse pride, that all but one of my chosen fallacies (that on rent controls) move in the most respectable circles. They are to be found in the most solemn utterances of ministers and Chancellors, in the speeches of the members of both Houses, and in the leader and correspondence columns of *The Times, The Economist* and other famous newspapers. With one exception, which was not to be resisted, I have forborne from giving detailed references for each fallacy, as I originally planned to do. For it soon became clear to me that it would be quite unfair to do so. The fallacies are not 'stupid' fallacies, not even careless fallacies. They are all plausible, and an intelligent student of events can be forgiven for believing them. In any case they are so common as to make documentation superfluous labour. A person must be very shut off from the world not to recognize the bulk of them.

Before ending, I should perhaps assure the reader who is strong for 'realism' that I am fully aware of my academic way of broaching problems – the let-us-suppose-this and the let-us-imagine-that way of arguing. The reader may at first be inclined to jib at what may seem excessive simplification or deliberate evasion of the complexity of the real world. If one were engaged in describing the real world, or tracing the evolution of its institutions, such misgivings would be warranted. But since valid economic conclusions can be inferred only from relevant generalization about economic behaviour, and since in economics relevant generalization is impossible without drastic simplification, this way of going about things in economics cannot be avoided. Economic analysis does indeed strike one, at first sight, as being a somewhat anaemic and unpromising animal. But with patience and proper treatment it can be made to 'deliver the goods'. And the goods to be delivered in this volume purport to be a clearer and more sophisticated understanding of economic events than can be gleaned by the reader from current commentary in newspapers, magazines, and over the air.

*

My debts are many. I cannot hope to record the contributions of all members of the profession who, in some particular,

Preface

helped to clarify my mind on some aspect of a problem. Nor can I do more than pay a general tribute to those colleagues and students at the London School of Economics who have indirectly promoted this venture. More ideas than one can hope to trace arise out of informal discussions in seminars and in senior common rooms.

But the direct contributions made by several people call for special mention. My wife's initial and persistent incomprehension of economic matters provided a challenge that few economists have to face. If I have realized my full potential as a popular expositor of arcane matters the credit will largely be hers.

Certain of my colleagues generously gave up their very limited spare time in order to scrutinize various parts of the original manuscript. Mr Lawrence Harris, of the London School of Economics, gave me the benefit of his reflections on a couple of papers relating to prices and productivity. Dr Peter Oppenheimer of Christ Church, Oxford, cast his expert eye over the several papers relating to international trade, and uncovered a number of ambiguities and important omissions. Dr Lionel Needleman of Sussex University tackled a half dozen of the more ambitious papers at the last minute as a result of which I was able to make significant improvements in the exposition.

I had hoped that Mr Kurt Klappholz of the London School of Economics, who has written the introduction, would agree to become co-author of this volume. But the pressures on his time, arising out of his new duties at the School, defeated my hopes. Notwithstanding this disappointment, I have enjoyed many of the advantages of working with a co-author. For his kindness was such that he readily agreed to discuss each and every paper with me. I am heavily in his debt for countless criticisms and suggestions which, along with those of my three colleagues mentioned above, have contributed substantially to whatever merit the volume possesses. Finally I must record my appreciation of the services of Mrs D. Herman and Mrs D. Ireland of HIRASEC, who received from me a batch of papers with scribbled corrections and countless addenda, and presented me a

16

few days later with a flawless manuscript, and my indebtedness to David Thomson for uncovering a multitude of minor stylistic blemishes.

May 1968   E.J.M.

Introduction *by Kurt Klappholz*

I

In the following pages Dr Mishan endeavours to show that a number of widely held views on economic problems are fallacious. According to *The Concise Oxford Dictionary* a fallacy is a 'misleading argument, sophism, flaw that vitiates, syllogism ... delusion, error'. Thus, in one sense at least, 'fallacy' refers to logical errors. Indeed, in many of his attempts to expose the fallaciousness of certain views Dr Mishan concentrates heavily on their logical flaws. For example Dr Mishan points out that, if they are to be *consistent*, proponents of the view that an increase in the national debt imposes a 'burden' on future generations would also have to argue that any failure of the government to increase the current rate of investment similarly imposes a 'burden' on future generations. Yet this does not appear to be their view; hence they would seem to be inconsistent – and consistency is a matter of logic.

For an argument to be acceptable it must be free from logical errors. Logical errors are comparatively easy to discover, yet their absence does not guarantee the truth of an argument. For example, from the two premisses

(*a*) 'All men are immortal'
(*b*) 'John is a man'
it follows that
(*c*) 'John is immortal'.

The logic in this example is unimpeachable, but both the major premiss and the conclusion are false. Many, if not most, debates in economics relate to the truth or falsity of certain propositions which may be the premisses or conclusions of an argument. Examples of such propositions are: 'An increase in income-tax

19

Introduction

rates reduces incentives to work'; 'Devaluation improves the balance of payments'; 'Incomes policy is effective in stopping or reducing inflation'. Whether or not these propositions are true cannot be decided by logic alone and, if they are false, they are also fallacious. We must therefore turn to the question of how to decide what is true or false in economics.

II

It is, of course, notorious that economists and politicians hold different views on a number of topical issues. Indeed, one might argue that the differences between party political platforms derive at least partly from different views concerning the consequences of particular economic policies. Thus the old question arises: why should disagreement on such strictly scientific problems persist? Political parties continue to disagree about the specific *factual* consequences of high taxes, 'planning', reductions in tariffs, etc. They do not similarly disagree – indeed, as political parties they have no views at all – on analogous problems in physics or chemistry (no political party has yet announced that, in its view, a man can fly by flapping his arms!). Why, then, is there so much disagreement regarding the predicted consequences of taking particular actions in the domain of any of the social sciences? Some people would answer that the reason for this is that the kind of propositions listed above are simply not scientific; that whether one believes them to be true or false depends on one's 'ideology' or 'values'. Since different people have different 'ideologies' or 'values', they can never agree on the truth of such statements. This view is mistaken, despite frequent assertions to the contrary. Clearly the question 'How does the levy of a tax on the development value of land affect its market price?' is on all fours with any other question regarding the effects of a particular experiment.

As is well known, natural scientists try to answer questions about the working of the universe by performing an experiment and observing whether or not its outcome conforms with their

20

predictions. Thus, over time, disagreements are resolved and attention is turned to new problems. It is generally agreed that there is no substitute for this method of resolving scientific problems. If such questions as 'Is full employment compatible with stable prices?'; 'Does capital punishment act as a deterrent to murder?' are to be answered satisfactorily it is necessary that we check our predictions about the effect of full employment on prices, or of capital punishment on murder, against appropriate observations.

One reason disagreements tend to persist among economists is the difficulty of conducting controlled experiments in economics. The difficulty may be put as follows: predictions deduced from economic theories are, in general, subject to the 'all-other-things-equal' clause. Thus, when considering the effects of a tax on the development value of land we usually abstract from other changes, e.g. population growth, inflation, changes in building techniques, which may also affect the price of land. Scientists performing an experiment, say, to investigate the behaviour of bodies in a 'free fall', can do much to exclude the disturbing influence of atmospheric pressure; economists cannot similarly exclude the effects of technological change. One must not, however, exaggerate the difference between the natural and social sciences in this respect. The inability to keep 'other things equal' would not, in itself, be a serious source of difficulty provided we knew (a) how the 'other things' changed, and (b) how such changes affect the things we are interested in. For example, suppose we predict that the levying of a development tax will, by itself, have no effect on the price of land but it so happens that, simultaneously with the imposition of the tax, there is a change in building techniques. If we knew how that change in building techniques would affect the price of land, we could make allowance for it in predicting the effects of the tax. Usually, however, we do not have this knowledge, and we cannot then make a prediction that takes into account the change in building techniques. This helps to explain why the *thought experiment* has been so prominent in economics, and will feature frequently in the following chapters. It must be stressed once again that the 'thought experiment', which consists in tracing the logical consequences of certain assumptions regarding individuals' behaviour, is no substitute for the checking of conclusions against observations; as was illustrated above, flawless logic is no guarantee of truthful conclusions. There is, notwithstanding, some advantage in arriving at one's conclusions by a coherent argument, in particular when considering the logical consequences of different assumptions, as this is one way by which fallacies can be exposed.

III

It is perhaps fair to say that most people are interested in economics only, or largely, because of its bearing on governmental policies. So far, disputes about policies have been ascribed to disagreements about their expected consequences. It may be argued, however, that disagreements about policies would persist even if there were complete agreement about their expected factual consequences. This is so for the simple reason that most policies will affect differently different groups of people. American farmers might, for example, be in complete agreement with city-dwellers about the expected consequences of the abolition of farm price supports; but this would not necessarily lead farmers to support their abolition. However, no 'interest group' will openly proclaim that it is in favour of a policy which will benefit it at the expense of other members of the community! Instead, it will produce 'sound economic arguments' to the effect that its interests, and the public interest, coincide. Since we know that the interests of different groups often conflict, the use of this ploy by each inevitably arouses suspicion about the 'soundness' of the arguments employed. In these circumstances one may be forgiven for reaching the conclusion that the economic analysis which apparently forms part of such specious arguments is itself no more than special pleading.

Granted that economic arguments are often used to lend support to conflicting policies, must we conclude that economics is little more than the rationalization of particular interests? Such a conclusion, would, of course, be unwarranted, since any argument that can be used can also be abused. But it is as well to consider whether, and in what way, differences in material interests or in ideologies may influence the conclusions of an economic argument.

One important point needs to be made immediately. I just spoke of people using economic arguments to support the case for certain policies. If by 'economic arguments' we mean – as is usually meant – statements about the expected factual consequences of certain policies, then, *from these arguments alone,* no case for or against any policy can be made. As philosophers say, from what *is,* nothing whatever follows (logically) about what *ought* to be. As far as I know, most economists accept this philosophic position. However, if this were all that could be said about the relationship between economics and economic policy, our discussion would have to end at this point with a very simple observation: economics tells us what is – or, more correctly, *what we think is* – the case; from what is, nothing whatever follows about what ought to be done. Since economics, as such, tells us nothing about what ought to be done, it cannot be said to harbour any ideological biases.

This view is much too simple-minded, however, and we may usefully consider, in a general way, how a person's 'ideology' may influence his economic arguments.

Let us quickly dispose of a point which is exemplified in Dr Mishan's discussion of the alleged 'burden' of the national debt. The point is this: economists often use words in a technical sense which, in everyday language, have strongly emotive connotations. For example, economists define 'efficiency' in a technical sense and, on the basis of this definition, often come to the conclusion that monopoly, or restrictive practices, or tariffs, lead to 'inefficiency'. As we have just argued, from such conclusions it simply *does not follow* that monopoly or restrictive practices or tariffs are undesirable. But the public at large, overlooking this point, tends to regard 'efficiency' as something which *ought* to be promoted, 'burdens' as something which *ought* to be avoided, and so on. Hence it is often argued that, despite protestations to the contrary, economics does tell us what we ought to do, and hence is clearly ideological. Preceding remarks sought to show that this view rests on a logical error, although it may be admitted that it would be better if economists tried to purge their vocabulary of its more emotive terms. Even so, it must be stressed that the presence of emotive terminology need not bamboozle anyone. If some economist proclaims that 'full employment, inflation and tariffs lead to inefficiency', and the listener is tentatively in favour of all three, all he need do is to ask our hypothetical economist to explain more clearly what he means by 'inefficiency'. The listener can then decide whether 'inefficiency' in *that sense* is something he wishes to avoid.

A concrete example will easily show that the use of emotive terms need in no way inhibit critical discussions. In the U.S.A. the term 'socialist' carries strong emotive overtones – what is 'socialist' tends to be regarded as bad. Many people in the U.S.A. object to proposals for some kind of National Health Service on the ground that it would be 'socialist' and hence incompatible with the American way of life. If someone raises such an objection, we could ask him what he means by 'socialist' in this context; the answer would have to be that 'socialist' means that medical services would be provided to consumers free of charge, or at any rate at a price below cost, the subsidy required being financed out of taxation. If that is so, then the American pre-university educational system is also clearly 'socialist', even though it is regarded as very much a part of the American way of life. Thus, assuming our hypothetical critic approves of the American educational system, we could immediately tell him that his objection to some kind of National Health Service cannot be *solely* that it would be 'socialist'. If he remains opposed to state subsidization of medical care, he has to provide other arguments.

IV

We may now turn to examples in which a person's ideology may influence the form of his argument. These examples hinge on the 'other-things-equal' clause.

A classic example is the way the notion of 'causes' is sometimes employed. How often have we heard it said that '*the* cause
of inflation is excessive government expenditure', or '*the* cause
of the U.S. balance-of-payments deficit is military expenditure
abroad'? How may someone who, for example, is against inflation but in favour of high government expenditure counter
such views? Or must he give up either his support for the latter
or his opposition to the former?

First, it should be understood that even if there were a single
or main cause, it does not follow that the single or main remedy
is the removal of that cause. Indeed, a knowledge of 'causes' is
not always necessary, or even relevant, in proposing a remedy.
To take a trivial example: if we are told that the cause of a man's
destitution is the loss of his arms, which renders him unfit for
work, it does not follow that the *only* remedy is the restoration
of his arms. More generally, whenever we are confronted with a
situation which we wish to remedy, say, poverty, inflation, a
balance-of-payments deficit, the relevant question is not: 'What
is the cause of the situation?', but rather, 'What are the alternative ways of dealing with it?' Of course, if there is only one way
of remedying a situation there is little to be said; but this is not
generally the case in the kind of problems with which economics
deals.

To revert to our example that government expenditure is *the*
cause of inflation. While a reduction in government expenditure
is one way of mitigating inflation, no one would seriously
suggest that it is the only way. What, then, can be meant by saying that government expenditure is *the* cause of inflation? One
sense is that mentioned above in connection with the man who
suddenly becomes destitute as a result of losing his arms: until,
say, last month, there was no inflation, then the government
increased its expenditure, thus increasing demand in the economy
and setting off an inflationary movement. This is clear enough,
but it in no way suggests that government expenditure should be
reduced in order to halt the inflation, unless (*a*) this is the only
way of achieving that aim (which we regard as overriding all
other aims) – and we have suggested that this is hardly ever the

25

case; or (*b*) government expenditure is less useful to the community than other forms of expenditure, in which case it should be cut irrespective of inflation.

It remains to consider more explicitly how these considerations are relevant to the 'other-things-equal' clause. What we are about to say has been implicit in the foregoing discussion.

The arguments about the 'causes of unemployment' in the 1930s provide an apt example. In the context of the theories which economists had in mind* it could be shown that (ignoring foreign trade), if the quantity of money in the economy were held constant, an increase in money wages over a short period of time would reduce the level of employment, and a cut in money wages would increase it. Accepting a fixed quantity of money as part of the 'other things equal', it could be said that too high money wages were 'the cause' of unemployment. The fixed quantity of money, however, is not a constant fixed by God or nature, but, on the contrary, can be altered by deliberate policy measures. It is held constant only as part of our mental experiment. If, instead, we allowed the quantity of money to vary, but in the new mental experiment held money wages constant, then an increase in the quantity of money would raise the level of employment, while a reduction in the quantity of money would reduce it. With this 'other things equal' – in this case fixed money wages – it could be said that 'the cause' of unemployment was too small a quantity of money.

Now the two ways of increasing employment, i.e. by cutting money wages or by increasing the quantity of money, will have different effects on the price level. By cutting money wages, an increase in employment would be secured with a lower price level than if the same increase in employment were brought about by an increase in the quantity of money, money wages remaining fixed. Hence, those opposed to a higher price level might be inclined to treat *the quantity of money* as among the

---

*The notion of 'cause' makes sense only in the context of a theory or law; 'we can never speak of cause and effect in an absolute way, but ... [only] ... relative to some ... law'. Cf. K. R. Popper, *The Open Society and its Enemies*, third edition, Routledge, 1952, Vol. II, p. 262.

things to be held equal, and therefore regard high wages as the culprit; those less worried by a higher price level and more worried by workers' resistance to wage cuts might be inclined to treat *wages* as among the things to be held equal, and regard the deficient amount of money as the culprit.

Analogous remarks may be made as regards the analysis of, e.g., balance-of-payments deficits: those wedded to *fixed* exchange rates and *stable* prices (and not unduly worried by unemployment) may tend to hold these things constant in their analysis and therefore tend to regard inflation as 'the cause' of the deficit; *per contra* those strongly opposed to unemployment and less worried by inflation may tend to include full employment among the things to be held constant in their analysis and therefore to regard an overvalued exchange rate as 'the cause' of the deficit. In all these cases a difference in values, i.e. in the weights to be attached to the various aims of policy, may influence the way an argument is put by affecting the choice of things to be held constant.

v

Some writers urge that in order to mitigate this 'illicit' influence of 'ideology', economists discussing economic policy should engage in self-analysis in order to discover which of their arguments are prompted by their political values and which by their judgements of the facts. Honesty requires that they communicate the results of this self-analysis to their audience. Such a prescription is redundant and probably impossible to fulfil. It is impossible to fulfil because one's judgement of 'facts' is often coloured by one's values and vice versa. If the prescription is interpreted as demanding that economists state which of their policy conclusions follow from factual premises and which from value premises, the answer again is that they follow from both. The prescription is redundant because in any discussion a person's motives are utterly irrelevant; what matters are the arguments he puts forward. The way to avoid the misleading arguments which try to derive remedies from 'causes' is to remember that,

Introduction

when it comes to issues of policy, the problem is to make the best choice from among the courses of action open to us. If someone presents us with a number of choices none of which we like, we should bend our minds towards finding less objectionable alternatives.

VI

Those who agree with all of Dr Mishan's views may find this Introduction of little interest, since they will not wish to criticize him. It is therefore addressed principally to those who may disagree with some or all of his views.

The point of this Introduction is to suggest what are, and what are not, relevant disagreements or criticisms. If a reader found Dr Mishan committing a logical error, then this would indeed be a relevant criticism; similarly, if a reader thought that some of Dr Mishan's views on how the economy works are false, then this, too, is a most pertinent criticism (though it must always be remembered that *believing* something to be false does not imply that *it is*, in fact, false). Again, if a reader disagrees with Dr Mishan's views on desirable policies, e.g. his views on rent control, he should ask himself whether he can think of alternative policies which, on balance, can be expected to have more desirable consequences. However, one cannot relevantly criticize Dr Mishan's views on, for example, rent control, by claiming that he is merely an apologist for landlords, or by verbal quibbles about his particular choice of words. As Dr Mishan explains in his Preface, he hopes that his books will contribute to a more enlightened discussion of current problems of economic policy. The kind of irrelevant criticism I have just mentioned has no place in any enlightened discussion.

The London School of Economics   KURT KLAPPHOLZ

Part 1 Fallacies About Taxes and Controls

1 Rent Controls are Necessary during a Housing Shortage

'Landlords are taking advantage of
the current housing shortage to raise rents.'

I

This is a fairly moderate version of a popular protest against rising rents. It is not uncommon to read in some sections of the Press that landlords are 'exploiting' the situation by charging 'exorbitant' rents, or by 'rack-renting' the hapless tenant. Apparently the typical landlord is an unprincipled person who readily avails himself of the urgency of other people's needs to line his pockets.

Now, as those who listen fairly regularly to 'brains trust' programmes must have realized, one can gain a reputation for shrewdness in a very short time merely by asking colleagues to explain the meaning of the words they use. Like most useful gambits it can be overdone. In this instance, however, we are justified in asking that the term 'current housing shortage' be elucidated, for we are not likely to make sense of the behaviour of landlords unless we know more precisely the nature of the situation to which they are reacting.

We might, of course, interpret a housing shortage in the light of some ideal standard: for example 'Every family of four should have, at least, three bedrooms and two living rooms with a total of not less than 11,500 cubic feet of space. . . .' Such a norm sounds humane and reasonable. It might be prescribed by a conscientious social worker in the belief that it is not too far ahead of existing standards in most parts of the country. But it is obviously a very fleeting norm. A hundred years ago it would have sounded wildly extravagant. A hundred years hence, if population continues to expand, it may again sound wildly extravagant. But today there can be wide differences of opinion both as to what is desirable and as to what can be afforded.

The economist, however, can be very complacent about all

31

this. He need not stick his neck out on so controversial an issue. Without saying a word about ideal or desirable standards he can go on to talk about a shortage of anything in a perfectly unambiguous sense. To the economist there is a shortage simply if, at the existing price, the maximum amount that people want to buy – in this case, the use of house-room – exceeds the maximum amount that sellers are willing to put on the market at that price.

It must be admitted, in passing, that it is not always easy to measure the actual excess of the quantity demanded over that being supplied. For one thing, the goods in question may not belong to a homogeneous class. Houses, for instance, may be classified into broad or fine divisions according to the problem in hand. If we want to illustrate the working of broad principles, as we do here, there is an advantage in supposing that all houses are equally desirable so far as the public is concerned. We can, at a later stage, consider what modifications of our conclusions are necessary, if any, when we remove this simplification.

There are, again, difficulties about gathering data, as well as difficulties of interpreting the facts once we have them. If, for example, we observe that the prices of all types of housing are rising and we also have information that no additional housing has been provided, we might conclude that the rise in price will lead to a diminution of the excess demand. For as prices rise, people will not be able to afford as much housing. However, from the fact that house prices rise we cannot be certain that the excess demand is being choked off. For it is possible that, just at the same time as some people are seeking to buy less housing at the higher price, other groups want to buy *more* housing, either because of increased incomes or, possibly, because of increased migration into the area. And these additions to the total demand for housing may more than offset the reduction in demand of the first group. Thus, even though there has been a rise in price, excess demand is greater than before. With these new demand conditions – those arising from migration and higher incomes – the required equilibrium price may be much higher than before.

For all that, however, the economist's *concept* of a shortage –

the excess demand associated with a given price – presents no difficulty, and it is with concepts, and not their measurement, that we are concerned now.

The tendency, in the absence of government or other controls, for the price to rise when there is an excess demand at that price is a response which is taken as *axiomatic by economists. It is a response which may appear to the reader as intuitively reasonable. If, however, he is loath to rely merely on intuition (for which reluctance I have nothing but praise), he can infer as much from observing the trading that is done on the floor of any stock or commodity exchange. Though the response of prices may be more tardy and erratic in less organized markets, for instance the market for second-hand cameras, the proposition is no less valid.

self evident

It may be emphasized that there is nothing automatic about this price behaviour. Prices do not rise of themselves unwilled by man. They are deliberately raised either on the initiative of some of the sellers or of some of the buyers according to the custom of the market. It may thus be the literal truth that landlords raise their rents when, at the prevailing price of house-room, there is just not enough to go round. To that extent a fallacy does not inhere in the quoted statement *per se*. Nonetheless it does attach to an implied 'ought' 'in that statement. That is to say, there is an implication in the statement that landlords are misbehaving or breaking the rules in some sense. And it is in this implication that a misunderstanding, if not a fallacy, can be detected.

II

Let us be quite clear on this point before considering the consequences of attempting to restrain the landlords' behaviour in times of a housing shortage. The reader is not being asked to acquit the landlord of greed or even of 'undue' greed. He is being invited to believe that in business affairs greed is the rule and not the exception; indeed, that it is the mainspring of the market mechanism as it exists in the free enterprise systems of the West. At least as far back as Adam Smith economists have been making the assumption that each man pursues his own interest only. No doubt there are circumstances in business when it is not politic to appear too grasping. In large organizations, moreover, frequent alterations of price lists can be highly inconvenient. But for all that, we shall not go far wrong in our interpretation of business activities if we continue to suppose that a man will sell dearer if he believes he can thereby increase his present and future profits. 'Exploiting the market' or – that which sounds less offensive but comes to the same thing – 'charging what the traffic will bear' is accepted by economists as normal business practice. However, if we cannot condemn the reaction of landlords to a housing shortage without at the same time condemning the system of private enterprise,* we might yet take the view that in this particular instance a rise in the price would be unusually damaging and, therefore, that measures to inhibit the free play of the market mechanism are justified. We shall devote the remainder of this essay to an examination of this view.

Though the material consequences of rent controls are not difficult to trace, the passions which are aroused by this inflammatory topic make it troublesome to discuss in mixed political groups, large or small. Invariably, unless the chairman is very determined, the features of the various rent restriction acts come under attack by some and are defended no less vehemently by others. Experience in conducting such a discussion suggests that before allowing temperatures to rise, the participants agree to abstract from any legal or political issues associated with the rent acts and to regard the housing shortage as a commodity in short supply to which, in the first instance at least, general economic principles will apply.

If the reader suspects a retreat to an ivory tower, I assure him that he is right. It is only in this more rarefied atmosphere, untroubled by the detail and many-sidedness of earthly things,

*The working of the private enterprise system is subjected to some scrutiny in Chapters 6, 7 and 8.

Rent Controls are Necessary during a Housing Shortage

that one can gradually discern the broad features of the land-scape. The reader is therefore requested to follow me into this lonely retreat and to make himself familiar with its advantages since, indeed, we shall frequently resort to it in the following pages.

Let us forget then about the differences between types of houses and imagine a rise in rents steep enough to wipe out all excess demand, in the economist's use of that term. In the 'short run' – say, during the following year – we can ignore the building of additional houses, for they will be too small a proportion of the existing stock of houses to make much impact on rents. Rents during this period will therefore be above 'normal' – that is, above the existing costs of providing new house-room – and this rise in the price of house-room relative to the price of all other things acts to serve notice on the community that house-room has become scarcer, and that people must economize in its use. At the higher prices, as people do economize in its use – as they agree to occupy fewer rooms and to seek no longer (at the higher prices) to occupy a larger house or flat – the shortage (in the economist's sense) will disappear.

In the longer run, we attend to the effect on rents as the proportion of new houses coming on to the market grows. As we should expect, additional houses bring down the high price attained in the short run to the level of the normal price (which just covers costs of providing house-room), profits disappear, and there is no further incentive to increase the resulting stock of houses. We may then talk of the market for house-room as being 'in equilibrium', there being no tendency for the stock of accommodation or the price of house-room to change.

A centrally planned economy faced with a housing shortage would not be criticized if it exacted economy in the use of scarce housing, and also initiated a building programme to meet the current deficiency. In these respects, therefore, there is little fault to find with the repercussions of the market mechanism. Of course, if prices are not permitted to rise, we cannot expect people to further ration their consumption of house-room and

35

the shortage will continue. Moreover, if prices do not rise, profits are not made, and businessmen are not attracted into building houses. If houses are to be built, the government then must step in and build them.

III

But, cries some impatient reader, this ivory-tower business is all very well in its way, yet what of the hardship suffered by the poor when rents are allowed to rise without limit? Let me assure that reader that a tender conscience is no necessary handicap to the economist. Not only can we admit that a rise in the price of house-room bears harder on the poor than on the rich, as of course does a rise in the price of anything that is consumed by both groups, but we can contemplate doing something to alleviate this hardship. The real issue then becomes one of the best methods of achieving this desideratum. And since it was regard to equity that prompted us to think of rent controls as a means of helping the needy, we must consider, also on grounds of equity, the following points which may be raised against rent controls.

First, it is a blunt and indiscriminating weapon. There are poor landlords and there are rich tenants; at any rate, there are many landlords (and landladies) who are poorer than their tenants. In such cases – and they are far from few since, before the First World War at least, small house property was a favourite medium for the investment of small savings – rent controls may constitute a transfer of real income from the poor to the rich.*

Second, even if we supposed all landlords to be better off than their tenants, rent controls – which may be regarded as a compulsory subsidy from the landlord to the tenant equal to the difference between the controlled price and the estimated market price – discriminate against the owners of a particular class of property in an arbitrary manner. The discrimination is arbitrary

*See the relevant chapters in the Milner-Holland Report on Housing in the London area.

in two ways. One, controls are applied to housing but not in general to other goods and services. Two, the controls are not symmetric. If the government also fixed *minimum* rents when rents would otherwise fall, landlords would feel less free to grumble. As it is, landlords are freely permitted to lose money in times of too much housing but are not suffered to make any during a shortage.

Nor is it satisfactory to argue that such an arbitrary procedure be accepted as part of the inevitable hazards of private enterprise along with unforeseeable changes in consumers' tastes, in technical innovations, or in the political situation. The last three are risks which the businessman tacitly accepts. He has not yet accepted government intervention of this particular sort since, according to the prevailing political philosophy of the West at least, the business of the government is to alleviate hardship or misfortune that results from the operation of natural or economic forces; to promote equity, not to create inequities.

Broad principles by which income is transferred from the community to the government both for its direct needs and for distribution among the poor have already been accepted by the community. Each contributes according to his income, and according to his expenditure, on a scale laid down each year by Parliament. One may, of course, protest that the tax rates are too high or the incidence too progressive, but there is general acceptance of the basic principle: from each according to his income and expenditure. The burden of any additional help to the poor should on this principle therefore be borne by the tax-payers as a whole and not made a charge on a particular body of people merely because it is administratively convenient and politically popular to compel them to bear it.

If we accept these objections to rent controls, we might go on to propose that (*a*) only the really poor (defined in some socially acceptable manner) qualify for low controlled rents, and (*b*) the difference between the estimated market rent and the government controlled rent be paid by the government on behalf of the poor tenant to his landlord, the funds necessary to finance this subsidy coming out of the general revenues.

37

The letting of council houses at a rent well below the free market rent would seem to accord with these proposals. Those eligible to occupy them are working-class people and are supposed to be earning low incomes – though it is not unknown for combined family earnings to be well above the national average for families. And the subsidy is financed from the local revenues, the tax falling directly on all property-owners (with a part of it entering indirectly into the costs of goods and services sold within the rate-paying boundary). Nonetheless, even these more equitable arrangements are open to criticism on allocative grounds.

For one thing, if we subscribe to the doctrine that, in the choice of material goods at least, each person knows his own interest best, then it would be better to give these subsidies *direct* to the poor to spend as they wish. After all, any person will consider himself better off if he is given an annual sum of money to spend freely than if the sum is given to him contingent upon his spending it in a certain way.

For another, the subsidy which is tied to house-room has the disadvantage that those who receive it have less incentive to economize on scarce housing that they would have if, instead, they received a direct, or unconditional, subsidy. The direct subsidy, we must suppose, is calculated to enable them to rent at the higher (market) price the same amount of accommodation, if they wish it, as they enjoyed under the system of controlled rents. But many of them are more likely to choose to rent less accommodation if they have to pay the full market value and, therefore, to use some part of their direct subsidy in the purchase of other things. In so far as there results from this method of direct subsidy a reduction of the rooms they occupy and, therefore, a release of additional accommodation to the rest of the community, there will be some decline in the market price of house-room.

IV

So far, what we have said in connection with a housing shortage might equally well have been said in connection with a shortage

38

of any other good or service. However, there have been several features particular to all rent-restricting legislation which are worth looking into.

(*a*) Not all rents were subject to controls, but only those below a certain rateable value. There was, then, a free sector of the housing market in which rents could rise without legal prohibition.

(*b*) In the controlled sector, rents were fixed initially with reference to their pre-war level, and later on by reference to rents ruling at some earlier date. Since prices *in general* had doubled over the war period, and continued to rise over the post-war period, the level of these controlled rents, far from reflecting the relative scarcity of housing by rising somewhat higher than the general level of prices, did not rise at all, or rose only by a limited percentage permitted by subsequent legislation. In *real* terms controlled rents were a half, and later on only a third, of what they had been before the war.

(*c*) Many of the rents of flats or new houses, in particular of the more expensive kind of houses or flats, built after a certain date, were exempt from controls. This feature was clearly designed to encourage new building by private enterprise. In the event, private enterprise, not surprisingly, sought to invest in houses or flats to be let only to the middle class and the well-to-do. It was left to the councils to provide the bulk of the new working-class accommodation.

These three features issued in several undesirable consequences. First, since there was this very large difference between controlled and uncontrolled rents, a tenant fortunate enough to come under the terms of the act then in force knew that if he left his existing abode he would not be able to find a vacant rent-controlled house or flat – at least not without paying a prohibitive premium, or 'key money'. In effect, the condition of his continuing receipt of this subsidy was that he 'stay put'. In the immediate post-war period when, owing to the need for re-adjustment to a peace-time economy, a high mobility of labour was imperative, there was this strong inducement for a large part of the working population to remain where it was.

Second, as may be gathered from our remarks on the difference between a house-tied subsidy and a direct and unconditional subsidy, the larger the controlled sector of the market – the sector in which people have no incentive to economize on scarce housing – the greater the housing shortage, and therefore the higher the level of rents paid, in the uncontrolled sector.*

Third, owing to the exceedingly low level of rents, in the controlled sector landlords had little inducement to keep their premises in good condition. If there was any definite hope of their property being freed from controls in the near future, landlords might have struggled along to maintain the condition of their properties in spite of the fact that, more often than not, their return was substantially less than the current costs of depreciation and repairs. But until such assurances were forthcoming landlords took the view that any expenditure on their property (other than that which could not be avoided) was tantamount to throwing good money after bad. In the circumstances, a vast proportion of the nation's housing was left to deteriorate rapidly at a time when there was something of a housing famine.†

v

Before we summarize our findings, let us dispose of one common misapprehension: that rent controls prevent inflation. The argument runs as follows: since rents enter heavily into the cost of living, a rise in rents would lead quickly to a demand for higher wages by the unions which would raise current costs and, therefore, current prices.

If this argument were correct, there would seem to be a case in equity for holding down the prices not only of house-room

*In a technical paper which appeared in *Economica* (February 1967), Messrs Gould and Henry are interpreted as showing that this conclusion does *not* necessarily hold. But it does hold if we assume (as is reasonable here) that few people buy more than one home.

†Many of these points are argued ably and in greater detail by Dr Lionel Needleman in his excellent book *The Economies of Housing* (Staples Press, 1965). See especially pp. 162–7.

but of all other things too. Rather than have landlords subsidize their product to the tune of some fifty to seventy-five per cent, why not instead have *all* commodities and services subsidized by their producers to the extent of something between ten and fifteen per cent? However this may be, the argument is weak at three points.

(*a*) If, in fact, all rents were allowed to rise freely, wage-earners and other people would be spending a great deal more on rents and, to that extent, less on all other goods. The additional amount they would have to spend on rents represents, of course, additional income to the landlords who could, if they chose, buy up those goods and services which the rest of the population now have to forgo. However, if the landlord class is more thrifty than the other classes in the community, in particular the wage-earning class – and this is taken to be a fact by economists – this transfer of income from the rest of the community to landlords would result, on balance, in a reduction of aggregate demand and would therefore contribute to an easing of the existing inflationary pressure.*

(*b*) It is not to be imagined that the wage-earner is ever short of a reason for tabling a claim for increased wages. Any belief that if deprived of this particular reason they are unlikely to agitate for wage increases is politically naïve. A good union-leader will make serious attempts to wring concessions from an employer only if he believes there are good prospects. If the chances of getting a rise are known to be slight, extreme measures are not likely to be resorted to.

(*c*) The opportunity for raising wage rates will depend not only on the attitude of the industry, it will depend also on the attitude of the government through its ultimate control of the banking system. The industry may be quite prepared to grant wage increases in the belief that the increased costs can easily be passed on to the public, but if the government pursues a

---

*Whatever the causes of the existing inflation, a reduction of excess demand will act to ease the inflationary pressure. The effect on the cost-of-living index – which is associated with 'wage-push' inflation (see Chapter 3) – is discussed in the following two paragraphs.

policy of monetary stringency, some firms first, and sooner or later all, will just not be able to pay higher wages. The banks will not be able to lend them the additional money necessary to meet higher wage bills. Indeed, the banks will be calling in their loans rather than expanding them.*

VI

Let us conclude; in general, a shortage of any good in the economist's sense causes its price to rise. This acts to compel people to economize in its use and at the same time makes it profitable for private enterprise to increase the supply. If, as a consequence of a steep rise in price, poorer people suffer hardship a neater and more equitable way of alleviating this is by direct cash transfers from the general revenues. The alternative policy of holding down rents leads to socially undesirable consequences. Many tenants are made better off at the expense of their poorer landlords, and landlords as a class, instead of the community at large, are made to subsidize a large proportion of the community's tenants. In addition, rent controls have served to reduce the mobility of labour at a time when it is believed that it needs urgently to be increased, to discourage private investment in working-class accommodation, and to cause a rapid deterioration in the existing stock of rent-controlled housing.

We have not discussed the administrative feasibility of direct subsidies to the poor, though clearly this would have to be taken into account in any such scheme. My opinion, for what it is worth, is that the method of direct subsidies would be far less costly than the system of rent controls with which we are familiar. It would certainly entail less social friction and require none of the cumbersome legal machinery set up under the rent restriction acts.

As for political issues, it might be urged that rent-restricting legislation is relatively easy to enact. It has more popular appeal, being commonly understood by the greater part of the electorate as a 'Robin Hood' measure to help the poor. But it

* See Chapter 3, Section IV.

will be a sad day for the community when the economist, or any scientist for that matter, takes it to be any part of his task to promote or justify a policy on the grounds that it is 'practical policy'. His task is to point out to the community, as clearly as he can foresee them, the material implications of the alternative policies from which it can choose. This task, if discharged honestly and effectively, will itself modify and mould public opinion. Ultimately, it will make practical policies of greater wisdom than can prevail in a state in which the economist uses his expertise to sanction the political demands of an uninformed public.

2 Payroll Taxes Promote the Use of Labour-saving Machinery

*'A general payroll tax would provide an incentive
to use more labour-saving machinery, so promoting
increased productivity.'*

I

Proposals for a payroll tax based on the above facile reasoning
were in high vogue in the early 1960s. Such proposals still exert
an influence on those ready to believe that only a simple tax
device is needed to bring about the economic millennium. But,
to strike a sceptical note from the start, what is the justification
for the belief that a shift towards *labour*-saving machinery*
provides an impulse towards faster economic growth? Why, for
instance, should we not encourage a shift towards *capital*-
saving machinery? Better still, perhaps, we should try to encourage a shift towards both labour-saving and capital-saving
machinery by taxing both labour and capital!

Before working up excitement over the possibilities, however,
let us pause to consider one obvious but unattractive consequence.
The most significant feature of a good pricing system is that the
relative scarcities of the basic resources available in the economy,
e.g. land, labour and capital, are properly reflected in their relative
prices. These relative prices act as guides to industry in their
choice of techniques of production. If labour goes up in price
as a result of an increased scarcity, industry will find it profitable
to economize on labour by choosing methods of production that
require less labour than before.† If, however, the price of labour

* Labour-saving *inventions* would, of course, be welcome. But it is
doubtful whether a tax on labour could encourage the invention of specific
labour-saving devices. Capital-saving inventions would, of course, be no
less welcome, though nobody has yet suggested that a tax on capital will
bring this about.

† Consumers, too, have an inducement to contribute to this economizing
on now scarcer labour. Since the costs of those goods which use more
labour than is used on the average will rise relative to the costs of all other
goods, consumers will reduce their purchases of the former – the 'labour-
heavy' goods – in favour of the latter.

44

Payroll Taxes Promote the Use of Labour-saving Machinery

is raised by levying a stiff tax on its employment, the higher price to industry will indicate that it is scarcer than it really is. Producers will then attempt to use labour more sparingly in relation to machinery – or, put the other way round – will attempt to use capital as though it had become abundant in relation to labour. But this is not only unwarranted: for the economy as a whole it is not possible. To illustrate, let us suppose the amount of capital to be given, and further, let us suppose that a tax on labour *could* make labour appear dearer in relation to the price of capital (we shall look into the question of *whether it could* below). In producing the same goods and services as before, the industrial system will attempt to use less of the 'dearer' labour, attempting to substitute machinery for it. If, as we assume, the economy is fully employed, the now smaller demand for labour will be smaller than the labour force in existence. In contrast, the new capital and machinery requirements will be greater than the existing stock of capital goods. It takes a lot of time for unemployed labour to die off, and time also for the capital stock to grow – especially now that the relative price of capital goods has apparently fallen. The unemployed labour will, over time, tend to depress wages. Excess demands for capital goods will, on the other hand, tend to raise the price of capital goods. In short, such intervention tends to be self-defeating: it creates a redundancy of one resource, labour, which acts to lower its price. At the same time it creates a shortage in the supply of the other resource, capital, which obviously acts to raise its price. These opposite price movements themselves tend to restore the original prices of the factors which properly reflect their scarcity.*

*If we want to generalize, we could say: given people's tastes, the distribution of their purchasing power and full employment of resources – that is the full employment of all the existing types of labour, capital and land – implies a given set of prices for each of these resources. Any attempt to alter these resource prices directly – by 'artificially' adding to one of their prices or subtracting from the price of another – will set up tendencies to restore their original prices.

II

Before dissecting the main fallacy in the quotation above, an auxiliary query comes to mind in connection with this proposal for a payroll tax. Suppose it were effective after all, at what rate should it be set? For if, say, a ten per cent payroll tax led to a rise in the growth rate by one per cent, why not push this button a little harder? Why not a fifty per cent tax; indeed, why not a 500 per cent tax? A 500 per cent tax should really have us ripping along the growth path! If proponents of the tax demur, let them explain. Or, better still, let them explain the principles that will determine the 'optimal' payroll tax. Whatever it is, we should have no difficulty in selling the idea to countries such as India or Egypt where the need for growth vastly exceeds our own.

Let us now turn our attention to the main fallacy: that a general tax on labour would induce manufacturers to shift to more labour-saving machinery. The naïve reasoning is, presumably, that a tax which raises the price of labour to manufacturers, and so raises unit costs also, provides an incentive to seek methods of production that use less labour than before – in short, to substitute machinery for labour. For this to be attempted at all, however, it is first necessary that the price of labour rise, and rise *relative* to the price of machinery. Clearly, if both the price of labour and that of machinery rise in the same proportion there will be no incentive for the manufacturer to substitute machinery for labour. As the reader may well suspect by now, this indeed is what happens. And it is not hard to explain.

Consider, first, the case of a tax that is a fixed percentage of the earnings of each worker – in the jargon, an *ad valorem* tax. By way of example, we can take an *ad valorem* of exactly 100 per cent and, for the simplest results, we shall provisionally suppose that the 100 per cent payroll tax comes into force without warning and is expected to remain in force indefinitely.

The long-run effects present no problem if the reader agrees that the costs of producing all goods or materials or machines can ultimately be decomposed into payments to the contribut-

Payroll Taxes Promote the Use of Labour-saving Machinery

ing 'agents of production': broadly speaking, into labour costs and interest charges.* The unit costs of all goods in the economy, including the costs of all machines, will all rise by 100 per cent provided, always, that the interest paid on borrowed money, say five per cent per annum, remains unaltered. And this is true irrespective of the proportion of labour used in the production of different goods.

Let £150 of good *A* be made up of £140 of labour plus £10 of interest charges (five per cent per annum on borrowing £200-worth of machinery necessary to its production). If, now, as a result of the 100 per cent payroll tax, the cost of labour to the manufacturer is doubled, then the same amount of *A* will

---

*If people agreed to lend money free of interest charges, the only costs involved would be labour costs. These labour costs might continue to exist even in conditions of natural abundance. Timber may be plentiful, but firewood will not be costless unless men are willing to give away the wood they have chopped up and gathered together. Apples may grow wild, but unless people are ready to gather them and carry them to the market for nothing, apples in the market will cost something.

As for interest payments, if the amounts that some people want to borrow *exceed* the amounts that other people are willing to lend without charge, some positive rate of interest will emerge. And this positive rate of interest can become a part of the costs of production if some time must elapse between the paying out of wages and the sale of the finished product.

If, say, the demand for apples that at present grow wild becomes so great that their price on the market exceeds the cost of labour involved in bringing them to the market, there will be an incentive to plant new apple trees. Planting trees may require clearing the ground and tending the young trees. Someone will have to pay wages regularly for, say, five years before the trees yield any fruit, and the investment begins to pay its way. Even if the businessman has money of his own, and does not have to borrow, he will, as a matter of course, enter interest at five per cent into his costs. For he can always lend his money elsewhere at the market rate of five per cent.

The cost of the finished product can only resolve itself into the two sources of costs: payments to labour and payments to 'capitalists'. We could have introduced a third contributory agent, land, but there is no advantage in doing so. (The payment to land, *rent*, is 'price-determined' in the long run and can, then, be depended upon to rise in the same proportion as labour and machinery – by 100 per cent in our example – thus maintaining the same real value as before.)

cost £300, this £300 cost being made up of £280 of labour plus £20 annual interest charges on the cost (now) of £400 worth of machinery. The reader will readily grant that if the machine in question were produced entirely by unaided labour its cost must double. Yet the cost will double even if the cost of the machine were not unaided labour, but in part also interest charges on some other *B* machine necessary to the production of the *A*-producing machine. For example, if before the payroll tax the £200 cost of the machine was made up of £150 of labour plus £50 of annual interest on £1,000, this £1,000 being the cost of the *B*-machine, the levying of a 100 per cent payroll tax would raise the cost of the *A*-machine to £400. Of this, £300 would be for labour, and £100 would be the interest, at five per cent per annum, on the £2,000 cost of the *B*-machine. Of course some part of the *B*-machine may also be interest charges, but we can always carry the process back far enough to decompose the cost of machines that make machines that make machines into these two components, labour costs and interest charges, without altering our result.

The thing to notice is that the payroll tax leaves unchanged the proportion of labour cost to capital cost – in other words, the price of labour to the price of machinery does not alter. In our example of good *A*, the ratio of labour cost to capital cost before the payroll tax is £140 to £10; or 14 to 1. After the 100 per cent payroll tax, the ratio of labour cost to capital cost is £280 to £20; again 14 to 1.

In case the reader feels there is anything special about the 14-to-1 ratio, let us take another good *C* with a 7-to-8 ratio. Suppose then £150 of good *C* is made up of £70 of labour cost and £80 of interest charges (five per cent on £1,600 worth of machinery necessary to its production). A payroll tax of 100 per cent puts up the price of labour to £140 and puts up the interest charges to £160 (five per cent per annum on the cost of £3,200 worth of machinery). The initial ratio, of 7 of labour cost to 8 of capital cost, remains unchanged.

Clearly, then, increasing the price of labour alone does *not* increase the cost of using labour compared with the cost of using machinery. Both labour and machinery costs rise in the same proportion exactly, so there can be no incentive to substitute machinery for labour.

Introducing imports into the picture makes no difference. For in the long run a rise of all our money prices by 100 per cent has to be accompanied by a devaluation of sterling to half its foreign price (say from $2.40 for £1 to $1.20 for £1) in order to maintain the pre-tax balance of payments.

III

What of the short period? It may, for instance, be suggested that although the prices of new goods and new machinery are bound to rise by 100 per cent, the interest *payments* on the existing machinery being used happen to be fixed in amount and, being based on the *old* prices, are smaller than they would be on new machinery. For a short period, at least, the costs of consumer goods do not rise by the full 100 per cent, and therefore prices of such goods *need* not rise by 100 per cent. More relevant, however, the prices of the machines *currently* being produced may also not rise by the full 100 per cent. For some time must elapse before the machinery and plant being used wear out and the machine-tool industry encounters the higher costs of re-equipping itself. It may seem, then, that if the manufacturers of consumer goods act quickly they may secure new machines at prices which have risen less than 100 per cent.

Nobody can say this is impossible. But even if this happens for a time, the manufacturers of consumer goods would not be able to use these newly bought machines for producing consumer goods with less labour than before. New kinds of labour-saving machinery (though of kinds that are already known to be technically possible) will first have to be designed to take advantage of the apparently lower costs of machinery as compared with the costs of labour. But according as the machine-tool industry does begin to renew its existing equipment, the full 100 per cent rise in costs of machinery must (as indicated in the preceding section) be encountered.

Turning once again to imports, there will be a short period, prior to exchange-rate adjustment, during which there will be incentives to substitute foreign goods generally for the new higher-priced domestic goods, including therefore some substitution of foreign machines for domestic machines. During such a period, while the country's excess imports are causing a depletion of its reserves of gold and foreign currencies,* it may well be the case that some manufacturers, who would not otherwise have undertaken to produce certain goods, now avail themselves of relatively cheaper foreign machines to do so. However, we must note carefully that such a reaction is *not* an instance of substituting capital for labour. Foreign machines that are imported could just as well be capital-saving as labour-saving. Any device whatsoever that lowers foreign prices relative to domestic prices – and without any change in the price of domestic labour relative to domestic capital – will cause us to buy *both* more consumer goods *and* more investment goods (or machines) for as long as we are prepared to deplete our foreign reserves or increase our foreign indebtedness. And it is hardly necessary to observe that if we want more foreign machines than we normally import,† it would be more economic for the country to arrange to buy these additional foreign machines directly rather than to arrange matters so that, instead, we find ourselves buying a wide range of foreign consumer goods.

IV

Let us turn now from the discussion of a proportional payroll tax and consider, instead, a flat-rate tax of, say, £5 per week per employee. In the long run, wage costs will no longer go up in the same proportion throughout industry. For £5 per employee is a smaller proportion of the wage cost of a highly-skilled employee, earning, say, £50 per week, than it is of the wage cost of a rela-

* See Chapter 11.
† Such machines are not, in fact, any cheaper to the country than they were before: only the payroll tax in the short run (before the exchange rate is adjusted) makes them appear cheaper to the domestic producer.

tively unskilled employee earning, say, £20 per week. In the former case, it is only a ten per cent tax on the wage cost; in the latter case, the tax comes to twenty-five per cent of the wage cost. If it so happens that the machine-tool industry uses more skilled labour than the national average or, more precisely, if it pays higher wages than the national average, then the wage costs of that industry would carry a lower proportion of tax than that carried by industry as a whole.

As a result the per cent increase in costs of machine tools would be smaller than the per cent increase in the costs of all other goods taken together. In particular, the managers of the consumer goods industries, aware that machine tools were now cheaper than before as compared with (taxed) labour, will attempt to alter their methods of producing goods. They will look for ways of substituting machine tools for the now dearer labour. We conclude, therefore, that in the special case where the machine-tool industry uses relatively high paid labour, a *flat* rate of tax on all labour will lead to attempts to substitute more capital for labour in the consumer goods industries. This may well be the case in Britain. But if all we want is that manufacturers be provided with an incentive to use more machinery, it would be simpler to tax all labour that is *not* used in the machine-tool industry. It would, of course, be simpler still for the government to subsidize the prices of machinery directly – or through tax rebates for companies using earnings to buy machinery, or by reducing interest rates.

However, as we have already shown, any attempt to enforce prices of labour or capital that do not correspond with their relative scarcities in a fully employed economy sets up self-defeating tendencies. Even when we remove the assumption of a fixed labour force, or a fixed stock of capital goods, and allow, say, for capital accumulation over time, an unwarranted reduction of interest rates (or 'artificial' cheapening of capital goods) tends to increase current investment plans over available saving. In a fully employed economy this must add to the inflationary potential unless the government simultaneously increases taxes.*

* See Chapter 3.

3 Increased Taxation Adds to Inflation

*'Higher taxes raise costs and therefore prices.
Far from reducing inflation, they therefore add to it.'*

I

If any rise in prices were dubbed 'inflationary' then, by definition, a tax which raises any prices must be inflationary. But this definition does not accord with the popular understanding of inflation, which is that of a prolonged or persistent rise in the level of prices; moreover, one that is unwanted and unplanned. Inflation is thus associated with a failure of the economic mechanism. The inflationary economy, it is felt, is an economy that is not altogether under control.

These characteristics which serve to describe inflation do not, therefore, include a once-for-all tax-induced rise in the price of one or more goods. But if the apparent fallacy is settled by definition, we are still left with the more interesting question of whether the response to higher taxes will tend to warm up or to damp down an existing inflation. Thus, although it is true that the *initial* tax-induced rise in prices does not itself constitute an inflationary rise in prices, we have still to answer the more important question: does the subsequent response of people to this initial tax-induced rise in prices have the effect of adding further to the existing inflation?

We cannot start to answer this question, however, without first saying something about what the government does with the additional revenue it collects from the new taxes. For the government could use these additional sums of money either to buy goods, or to buy securities; or else it could in effect 'destroy' the money. Provisionally we can suppose the government follows the latter policy. The reader may, if it appeals to him, think of a stoker shovelling stacks of pound notes – the additional tax receipts – into a furnace. Alternatively he can think of the government putting the extra money it collects into cold storage.

Although the government in fact neither burns the notes nor freezes them, it could neutralize the monies just as effectively by recourse to more orthodox methods which will be described later. The important thing to bear in mind just now is that the government does not, in this case, buy anything with the extra money collected from the tax-payers.

II

The sorts of taxes relevant to this question are either *excise* taxes or *income* taxes; seldom capital or capital gains taxes. An excise tax is a tax levied on goods themselves at any stage in the productive or marketing process. Such a tax is not in general absorbed by producers – except perhaps in the very short run – but is reckoned by them as an addition to their unit costs and passed on to the public as such.* If only some goods are taxed, the public can shift some of their former expenditure on these now higher-priced goods towards other goods. But only if people respond to these new excise taxes by refusing to buy anything at all of these taxed goods will the government collect no additional revenue. In that extreme case the public would have the same command over resources as before:† the government would have failed completely to reduce the buying power of the public. Usually, however, the public will continue to buy some of the newly taxed goods, though less than before, and the government will succeed therefore in collecting some additional revenue. The government can, of course, put additional taxes on all goods. In that case the

---

*An exception to this rule would be a tax on products whose supply is fixed by the amount of land of a given quality. If the tax on such products were small enough, it would be absorbed wholly by the landlords and the price of the products would remain unchanged by the tax (see Chapter 4). Only in the limiting case in which the tax was so high that all the rents of the landlord could not suffice to pay it would the supply of the products be reduced and their prices rise.

†People would regard themselves as somewhat worse off, however, as they would prefer to buy goods at the prices existing before the additional excise taxes.

53

only way the consumer can legally avoid paying any tax is by not spending any money.

What about the effect of an income tax on buying power? Clearly if an addition to income tax is not compensated by a *fall* in product prices buying power is also reduced. The reader might wonder why an income tax, as distinct from an excise tax, does not add to costs and therefore raise the price of goods. The short answer is that it is absorbed by the tax-payer who does not respond by raising the price of his services accordingly. If every income-earner, regarded as a seller of services to the economy, did succeed initially in passing on the whole of the additional income tax to the public by immediately extracting from his employer a compensating rise in his money earnings then, indeed, we should be in trouble. For though his disposable money income has now been restored to its previous level, unit costs and, therefore, prices have been raised and his 'real' buying power reduced once more. Any additional increase in his money earnings will have the effect of raising prices still further. But we need not pursue the matter here since this does not seem to happen.* A rise in in-

* Why it does not happen is to be explained as much by conventions as by economics. It is true that there is little alternative open to an individual workman once income tax has been raised. Earnings in all other occupations are subject to the same rise in the tax structure. All there is left for him to do is to work fewer hours where possible and earn a yet smaller disposable income. But if employees *as a group* responded to a fall in their real disposable income when caused by a rise in the income tax as they now tend to do when it is caused instead by a rise in the prices, then, indeed, a rise in income tax would lead to a rise in prices.

In this connection it is interesting to speculate about the economic consequences of the growing mobility of labour between countries. A rise in income tax in this country may encourage emigration to countries where income tax is lower but where conditions are not too dissimilar. The more responsive people become to inter-country tax differentials, or to differences in real disposable income, the more will their incomes have to be adjusted to limit their migration abroad. In the extreme case, beginning with some equilibrium between this country and the United States, a rise in income tax in Britain would, in the absence of a similar rise in the U.S., presage a rise in costs and prices of some goods in Britain such as to restore the real disposable income differential between the affected category of earners in the two countries. In less extreme cases, the differential would not be wholly restored and we should lose some workers.

come, we may continue to believe, reduces disposable money income and does not raise prices. It reduces buying power directly.

We can, then, either lower disposable incomes (the income remaining after paying income taxes) without changing prices, or raise prices without changing disposable incomes, or we can do both. In sum, a fall in buying power requires a fall in disposable money incomes *relative* to prices.

Let us, however, concentrate on excise taxes, and for simplicity let us think in terms of a proportional rise in all excise taxes, say of fifty per cent, on all goods. In the first instance, with people's disposable money income unchanged, they can now buy only two-thirds of what they could previously: there is a fall therefore in the public's buying power of one-third. The crucial question is whether the tax-induced rise in prices will itself trigger off further changes. In particular, we should like to know whether the initial tax-induced rise in prices will give rise to compensating increases of income throughout the economy, so defeating the aims of the tax.

III

Now one cannot answer such questions without recourse to some theory of inflation. And the cynical reader will not be surprised to hear that there are two, somewhat opposing, theories of inflation. One is basically a 'demand-pull' theory. The other is a 'cost-push' theory. More searching analysis, along with the use of more sophisticated statistical techniques, may yet produce for us a mixture of the two theories which commands a consensus in the profession. In the meantime, and so long as the emphasis on the one theory or the other varies from one economist to another, we must consider in relation to our question the basic notion inspiring each theory.

A pure demand-pull theory would attribute inflation to excessive overall demand in conditions of 'full employment',* or

*'Full employment' is put in quotes since it is consistent with unemployment in some industries, along with a shortage of labour in other industries. Taking the economy as a whole, however, the number of vacancies is equal to or exceeds the total number seeking work.

near full employment – 'too much money chasing too few goods', so to speak. At any given moment of time, an economy in the throes of such an inflation will disclose an 'inflationary gap', which is measured at the existing price level by the excess of the value of aggregate expenditure over the aggregate value of production. This implies that the population as a whole (including the government) is trying to buy more goods than the economy is able to produce. Further, according to this view, the larger is the so-called inflationary gap, as a proportion of national income, the steeper will be the subsequent rise in money incomes and prices. Obviously, then, the remedy is to reduce the inflationary gap to nil; to reduce the buying power of the population as a whole so that, at whatever the resulting price level, it no longer exceeds the productive capacity of the economy.

This can be achieved in a variety of ways, not the least important of which is a reduction in total government expenditure – already, in Britain, equal to about half the total expenditure in the economy. And if we confine ourselves to the question, whether an increase in current taxes, and in particular a proportional rise in excise taxes, can reduce a pure demand-pull inflation, the answer is yes. The higher the excise tax, and the greater therefore the initial increase in per unit costs of all finished goods, the greater is the resulting shrinkage of buying power. We may safely conclude that if the inflation is caused wholly by excess overall demand, a rise in excise taxes large enough to soak up all the excess demand (the full amount, that is, of the inflationary gap) will bring the inflation to a halt – *provided* always that there is no offsetting source of increased purchasing power, such as an increase in the total supply of money.

Pure cost-push inflation, on the other hand, must be attributed to the attempt of workers as a whole to establish a 'real' wage in excess of that which emerges from the competitive process. So defined, cost-push inflation is consistent with any level of employment. If only half the workers in the economy are employed, an attempt to raise their 'real' wage above that determined by market forces initiates a cost-push inflation. A twenty per cent increase in money wages all round, if eventually granted, will add about twenty per cent onto costs and thus raise prices by about twenty per cent – so defeating the object of the exercise. Nevertheless, it is sometimes conceded that cost-push inflation begins to operate more strongly as the economy moves towards full employment which, as we have seen, is also the condition under which demand-pull inflation begins to assert itself.

Now if inflation is a pure cost-push phenomenon, a rise in excise taxes, which initially soaks up buying power, will fail to check it. For workers are trying to increase their 'real' buying power by raising their money wages. If the response of industry is to raise prices in the same proportion, wage-earners will have failed to raise 'real' wages. If, in addition, the government imposes excise taxes, raising prices still further, workers will demand a yet greater rise in their money wages to cover the extra cost of living. Once this is granted by industry, we are back at square one. For costs and, therefore, prices rise in about the same proportion. The desired 'real' increase in wages is as elusive as ever.*

Indeed, if a situation of *potential* cost-push inflation exists in a currently stable economy, the raising of excise taxes in the ordinary way, in order to pay for additional government expenditure, would have to be avoided. Imagine an economy in equilibrium and with no tendency for prices to rise. If the government now raises excise taxes to pay for some additional government expenditure prices rise and 'real' wages will seem to be lowered.†

---

*'Real' wages are limited by technology, total resource-endowment and, to a lesser extent, by economic institutions. Government intervention may be able to raise real earnings of small underprivileged groups by a significant margin through taxing the rest of the community. But some quick calculations with the figures presented in the tax tables should convince the reader that the wage and salary bill for the economy as a whole could not be augmented by more than a negligible proportion even if 'the rich' were subjected to prohibitive taxes. Higher 'real' earnings for the working population must depend ultimately on increased productivity.

†They would only *seem* to be lowered because we are discounting the value of the additional services which are to be provided by the government with the revenue it transfers from the tax-payer. A transfer of purchasing power from the private to the public sector does not necessarily reduce

The attempt of workers to restore 'real' wages by raising money wages, which further raises costs, is just the response needed to start off a 'wage-price spiral'.

Finally, if the inflation is recognized as being a mixture of both demand-pull and cost-push, excise taxes will also be ineffective. For if we begin with a situation in which the government has managed to squeeze out all the excess buying power in the economy so that, momentarily, the economy is in equilibrium, it cannot remain in equilibrium so long as some cost-push impetus is left. For any degree of cost-push implies that workers seek to raise 'real' wages in some degree above those corresponding to the existing productivity of labour. Their success in raising money wages is, therefore, necessarily accompanied by an overall rise in money costs and prices. 'Real' wages are back to what they were, and so the economy goes through the motions of chasing its own tail.*

IV

So far there has been a serious omission in our account of the matter – the question of the money supply.†

people's 'real' income; it may even raise their 'real' income. But people generally ignore government services when thinking of the buying power of their incomes.

*If workers initially demand, say, a twenty per cent rise in money incomes and then react to a subsequent twenty per cent rise in the price level by demanding a further increase in money wages, but *less* than twenty per cent, say fifteen per cent, what then? If they continue in this way, the economy will converge towards an equilibrium after a few twists of the spiral. The reader should also bear in mind that it takes time to negotiate wage increases covering the whole of industry, and time also to revise prices upward. In the meantime, labour productivity will be increasing, as a result of continued technological advance, so that aspirations towards higher 'real' wages can increasingly be met. But we speak only of possibilities. Knowledge of an increase in productivity may itself engender claims for yet further increases in 'real' wages. There is no evidence to support the view that only faster productivity can satisfy the demand for rising 'real' wages and so prevent inflation (see Chapter 19).

†It is sometimes alleged that 'Inflation is *not* primarily monetary in origin' – which presumably means that inflation is not caused, in the first

Increased Taxation Adds to Inflation

Popular expositions of the cost-push mechanism tend to omit any discussion of the supply of money; they make the tacit assumption that there are no checks whatever to the level of prices in the economy.* But if higher prices imply that more money is required to transact the same volume of business, continuous inflation will sooner or later 'exhaust' the existing amount of money in the economy. It can then continue only if the existing supply of money is increased, and continues to be increased faster than the growth of 'real' income so as to keep pace with the proportional rise in prices.

To illustrate, if workers as a whole demand, and receive, a fifty per cent increase in their money incomes, employers have to meet a weekly (or monthly) payroll that is fifty per cent larger. Where is this extra money to come from? At first, employers could use up, or 'activate', any spare cash and unused bank balances. These may not suffice and they may have to sell securities and other earning assets on the market. They will also

---

instance, by the government's expansion of the money supply (e.g. by buying bonds from the public). As Mr Klappholz has pointed out in his introduction to this volume, whether a particular act or policy is regarded as *the* cause, or one of the causes, of an observed economic phenomenon (inflation in this case), the remedy need not entail the removal of the alleged cause. There are generally several alternative remedial policies that may be employed to combat the undesirable effects in question. Thus, inflation may be caused by a combination of 'excessive' wage demands in certain sectors of the economy and/or aggregate 'excess' investment and/or 'excess' government spending and/or 'excess' consumer credit purchases – notwithstanding which it can be argued (and is argued) that firmer control of the money supply will act to restrain the pace of inflation.

* Sometimes it is briefly asserted that attempts to limit the supply of money cannot reduce inflation; that it can result only in bankruptcies and unemployment. Why this should be so, as distinct, say, from increasing taxes relative to government expenditure (which, as we have seen, may also entail a reduction in the money supply), has not yet been made clear. This view does not command consensus within the profession, and the empirical evidence of the United States would appear to support the view that changes in the volume of money do influence changes in the level of prices. The interested reader might wish to refer to a non-technical article by M. Friedman, 'The Role of Monetary Policy', *The American Economic Review*, March 1968.

turn to the banks for at least part of the extra money. The banks may be willing to accommodate them. But if not, employers may have to borrow from non-bank lenders at much higher interest rates. If the banks do not lend more money – and they will not be able to lend more if the Central Bank (the Bank of England in Britain) takes measures to prevent the creation of more money in the economy – the unused cash balances of employers and others are drawn into circulation in buying the same amount of labour and goods at higher prices. Once all the 'spare' cash in the economic system is used up in this way,* the inflation runs out of fuel and grinds to a halt. Thus, notwithstanding the willingness of employers to concede all demands for higher wages, if employers cannot raise increasing amounts of money to meet their rising wage bills, they will just not be able to meet these wage demands. The pre-condition of any sustained inflation, whether demand-pull or cost-push, is an accompanying increase in the supply of money. This continuous increase in the total supply of money has been a feature of the British economy since the war.† Without it the long period of creeping inflation could hardly have continued.‡

*This more intensive use of the existing stock of money in the economy (currency and bank balances together) is spoken of as an increase in 'the velocity of circulation' of the money supply.

†It is occasionally pointed out that not *all* of the annual increase in the money supply goes to support rising money incomes: a part is used to 'finance' Britain's current balance-of-payments deficit. This is based on the simple view that if Britain has a current excess of imports of, say, £250 million annually, there will be an annual net transfer to foreigners of an additional £250 million-worth of bank balances. But the whole of this sum is not necessarily held idle by foreigners, or exchanged for dollar balances at the Bank of England, and is therefore not necessarily 'immobilized'. To the extent that foreigners use a part of this sum to buy short-term securities the money is passed again into domestic circulation and, possibly, into the hands of those who may use it for current transactions.

‡Why did the government not combat inflation through a tightening of the money supply instead of conspiring to increase it (by buying bonds held by the public)? One cannot attempt to answer without broaching a controversial issue, one bound up with political views. Suffice it to say that some monetary economists of world reputation have emphatically condemned the government's economic policy in this respect. In this connection the interested reader might wish to refer to: Milton Friedman, *Capitalism and Freedom* (University of Chicago Press, 1963), Chapter 3.

V

We could, perhaps we should, end here. What follows is really an extended footnote to satisfy the inquisitive reader who wants to know a little more about what the government does with the tax proceeds it collects. So far we have been assuming that the government 'destroys' the extra tax revenue it collects. In fact, the government can 'neutralize' or 'sterilize' the extra tax revenues by leaving the extra money (transferred to its account by the public at large) in the bank. The government's current balance at the Bank of England is then increased, and it stays increased as the government does not spend any of it.

If the government wants the initial anti-inflationary impact of a given amount of additional taxes to be as large as possible it 'neutralizes' the tax proceeds: it leaves the extra money in the bank and does not spend a penny of it. If, in contrast, it spends all the extra tax proceeds on currently produced goods and services, the tax has no initial disinflationary effect at all. In fact this policy could be worse than doing nothing at all. Let us show this by an example. If the government withdraws £100 million from the pockets of its citizens and spends the lot itself, the expenditure of the economy as a whole (government and private expenditure taken together) does not alter *provided* citizens reduce their total expenditure by the full £100 million. But if instead they reduce their total expenditure by *less* than £100 million, there is a net increase of total expenditure. For example, if the public reduces its expenditure by only £90 million whenever it is taxed £100 million, and the government increases its expenditure by the full £100 million whenever it collects £100 million, the net increase of expenditure is £10 million.

As it happens people do behave like this. If their (disposable) incomes rise by £100 million they do not spend it all on domestic goods. They generally save a proportion, say ten per cent, and spend the rest.* If, on the other hand, their disposable incomes are reduced by £100 million, they behave in a symmetrical manner:

*A proportion is also spent on foreign goods, and to that extent is *not* spent on domestic goods.

they do not reduce expenditure by the whole £100 million, but only by £90 million.* And this being the case, if the government does spend the full proceeds of its taxes on currently produced goods, the net effect on overall expenditure is not zero. It is inflationary.

There is, however, an intermediate case between these two extremes. As an alternative to the government's spending on *currently produced* goods, it could spend the tax proceeds wholly on *assets* which exist already and which do not therefore make any demand on productive capacity. In particular, it could spend the tax proceeds on securities. More specifically yet, it could spend them on bonds, preferably on government long-term bonds held by the public. If the government does use the £100 million of its tax proceeds to buy bonds, the public will obviously be left holding £100 million more of cash in exchange for the bonds it has sold to the government. Will this sale of bonds to the government cause some increase in expenditure on currently produced goods to put against the initial reduction in current expenditure caused by the new tax?

The answer is yes if the government's bond purchases pushed up the prices of bonds, as is likely to be the case. If bond prices rise then their sellers make a capital gain, and being somewhat wealthier they respond by spending more on currently produced consumption goods. Increased current spending may also come from another quarter: for a rise in the price of bonds necessarily entails a fall in the interest yielded by the bonds.† And at lower interest rates it is cheaper for industry to borrow money to spend

*If people add to their annual savings by £10 million when their annual incomes rise by £100 million, then when their annual incomes fall by £100 million their annual savings are *reduced* by £10 million. People's consumption standards do not fall by the full amount of their incomes in the latter case; they are 'cushioned' by 'eating into' their annual savings.

†A newly issued £100 bond carrying a six per cent rate of interest in perpetuity entitles the holder to £6 per annum for as long as he holds the bond. A rise in its market price to £200 implies that anyone who now buys the bond pays £200 for a steady income of £6 each year. This works out at £3 per annum income for each £100 paid – a yield, therefore, of three per cent on his 'investment'. If the bond rose in price to £300, the yield would be two per cent. If it rose to £600 the yield would be one per cent.

on new plant and equipment. Those of the public who make a capital gain selling their long-term bonds to the government will spend, at the most, the full capital gain. This will be only a fraction of the £100 million they received for them. On the other hand, those firms who respond to a lower rate of interest by increasing their current spending on new capital goods and machinery might well increase expenditure by much more than a £100 million. If they do so, the net effect of the government's policy is inflationary.

However, existing studies indicate that the response of industry to the usual order of interest rate changes brought about by government purchases of long-term bonds is limited. We might tentatively conclude that using tax proceeds to buy bonds can be counted on to have some net disinflationary impact in the first instance, though not so large a disinflationary impact as can be expected from 'neutralizing' the tax proceeds.

This disposing of additional taxes by buying bonds is popular with governments, particularly with governments that have, over the past, sold large amounts of bonds to the public. The sum of these outstanding government bonds amounts to what is known as the national debt.* Whenever the government uses the proceeds of a 'budget surplus' – that is, the annual excess of taxes collected above its current expenditure – to buy back these bonds held by the public, it is said to be retiring part of the national debt. If over a long period of time successive governments generate budget surpluses and use them to buy up part of the national debt still outstanding, the whole of the national debt will eventually be retired. Though this is sometimes held to be a desirable objective of economic policy,† the reader is unlikely to see it realized in his lifetime.

VI

Let us summarize our conclusions.

If the inflation is a 'demand-pull' inflation – one arising from an

* In North America it is known as the public debt.
† Desirable because it is believed that the national debt imposes a burden of some sort on the economy (see Chapter 5).

overall excess demand in the economy – a rise in income taxes *or* a rise in excise taxes, either of which absorbs the excess purchasing power, will act to reduce the inflation; *provided*, always, that there is no simultaneous increase in the total money supply, and that the government does not spend any of the tax proceeds. If the government does spend the full amount of the tax proceeds on currently produced goods it will, on balance, add a little to the inflation. If, instead, it spends the full tax proceeds on government bonds the net effect is likely to be deflationary, though not of course as deflationary as not spending the tax proceeds at all.

If the inflation is a 'cost-push' inflation – one arising from widespread aspirations toward a higher level of 'real' earnings than is currently possible – a rise in excise taxes raises prices, lowers 'real' earnings, and so adds fuel to the inflation. And it does so irrespective of whether the government spends the tax proceeds or 'neutralizes' them. This conclusion depends, however, on there always being enough money available in the economy. A rise in the level of prices uses up money in paying higher incomes. Unless then the money supply is sufficiently increased, the inflation must eventually grind to a halt.

4 A Tax on Land Raises its Price

'Development potential of any piece of land
raises its market price and affords a capital gain
to its owner. But a tax on this resulting capital
gain will raise its price still further.'

If the reader is not already sceptical of the view that the economist has great influence in moulding public opinion, the Press discussion of the Development Levy introduced in the Budget of April 1965 should make him wonder. The Press gave virtually unanimous support to the above economic fallacy. And fallacy it certainly is according to current doctrine. No matter how much economists may disagree on a variety of issues, there will be a consensus on this one: and that is, that a tax on this capital gain of development land has no effect whatever on its market price.

The robust empiricist might suggest the question be settled by an actual experiment, by 'looking and seeing'. And, admittedly, there is no better method of seeking an answer to any question – provided always we can arrange the experiment. In economics the ideal experiment can never be tried. We could, of course, study events following the imposition of such a tax. But we cannot rely on the results simply because there would be other, and sometimes more powerful, forces at work which would also influence the phenomenon we are observing. For instance, the price at which land changes hands would be influenced, on the demand side, by the growth of population, by the growth in 'real' income *per capita*, by regional migration, by international trade, by technical innovations and so on. If we want to know just what difference it makes to the resulting price of land, we must somehow contrive to hold all other factors unchanged while we raise the land tax. This experiment can only be done in the mind of the economist: the time-honoured method of the 'thought experiment' in fact. Once we have finished thinking carefully about it, and come up with an answer, it may be possible to check our conclusion – to 'test the hypothesis' as scientists say. We should, of course, have to employ fairly powerful statistical techniques which make full allowance for all the other main forces affecting the price of land. But since we cannot in economics (as distinct, say, from chemistry or physics) hope to control the experiment so as to generate the data we want, we are at a disadvantage. We can only hope that relevant events over the past have been sufficient in number and diversity to throw up the minimum amount of data necessary to enable the economist to have confidence in the statistical findings. It must be admitted that the hopes of the economist in this respect are not always realized. Nevertheless, concerning this tax on the value of the development potential of a piece of land, there happens to be complete agreement among economists.

I

One rather obvious though perhaps minor effect of a levy on the capital gains that are made by selling land for development purposes is that of giving an incentive to sellers of land to mislead the tax authorities either by over-stating the current value of the land or by under-stating the development value, or both. This is not surprising. Dealers in land, like all businessmen, have an interest in misleading the inland revenue, and a new tax does no more than provide a new opportunity for doing so.* But it throws no light on the question at issue, which is the effect of the levy on the resulting price of land.

Let us consider a farmer who has obtained planning permission to develop one acre of agricultural land for residential purposes. The capital value of the land in its current (agricultural) use is, say, £400. How do we arrive at a figure for its development value? Planning permission usually specifies the 'maximum

---

*The Development Levy is imposed at the rate of forty per cent on the difference between the capital value of the land in its current use and its capital value after permission has been granted to transfer it to some other use – to 'develop' it in fact. (See Cmd 2771.)

permitted density' of development. Within the permitted limits, therefore, we may assume that the developer or builder who buys the land from the farmer will build the most profitable type of housing on it. To simplify the calculation, we suppose the builder can do best for himself by building a single house on this one acre of land. The building costs of such a house are, let us say, £6,000. If the land were free, there would be no other costs. He would then be satisfied to sell such a house for £6,600, ten per cent on cost being the normal profit. But building on this *particular* site he can, let us suppose, expect to sell the house for as much as £8,000. His anticipated profit, £2,000, is then in excess of his usual profit by £1,400.

Now this *extra* profit of £1,400 is the maximum amount the developer will be prepared to pay for the land.* This figure of £1,400 therefore represents the maximum value of the land for development purposes.

Now the farmer has only two courses open to him: he may keep the land in its present use or he may sell it for development. Provided the levy is less than 100 per cent on the new capital gain of £1,000 – the difference between its new development value, £1,400, and its existing agricultural value, £400 – he is sure to sell it for development if he is concerned only with increasing his wealth. As for the prospective buyer, the mere existence of a levy will not induce him to pay any more. For the levy, which has to be paid by the farmer, does not in the least affect the developer's building costs. Nor does it affect the maximum price that he can sell the house for, this price being determined by the demand for

---

*We have simplified further by tacitly (and incorrectly) assuming that the builder would still be satisfied with £600 profit. But once he has to pay cash for the land, this cash payment would really be added to his cost. If he wanted to make ten per cent on his *total* outlay, this total outlay must not exceed £7,273. (For ten per cent of this outlay is £727, which added to this total outlay brings the figure to £8,000, the price of the house.) The maximum development value is therefore the *difference* between the building costs of the house alone (£6,000) and the selling price of the house *after* deducting the normal profit on it (£7,273). This difference is therefore £1,273. For simplicity, however, we continue to take the figure £1,400 in the text.

housing, and therefore quite outside his control. The *excess* margin of profit for the builder is still £1,400, levy or no levy; nothing will induce him to offer more than that for the acre of land.

Since the levy does not affect the maximum amount any builder is willing to pay for this particular acre of land, we must conclude that the introduction of a levy does not raise the price of the land above that maximum. Like any other tax, a levy on the gains made by the seller will obviously reduce the amount of profit the seller finally pockets. If, for example, our farmer drives a hard bargain and gets the full value of his land, £1,400, forty per cent of this, £560, will have to be paid to the government. But the levy itself, whether forty per cent or ninety per cent, cannot raise the price of land above this figure of £1,400.*

II

The argument may be made clearer by entertaining some preliminary objections. Someone may protest that in the above illustration the acre of land was made to change hands at the maximum price that the developer was willing to pay, whereas in

---

*For simplicity of exposition we have assumed throughout that the seller, the farmer here, pays the tax to the government. But no modification to our conclusion is required if, instead, the buyer – here the builder – pays the tax. For just as the seller must subtract the potential tax before estimating his net profit on the sale of his land, so must the buyer when he himself pays the tax.

If, for example, the government suddenly changed the law so as to require the payment of the development levy to be made by the buyer, the £560 tax that the farmer had formerly to deduct from his capital gain would now have to be deducted by the builder from the selling price of the house he proposes to erect. In bidding for this acre of land in the open market, the most the builder would pay for the land alone would now be less by this £560 of anticipated tax payment. The farmer would then receive the value of his land *less* £560. But he would now no longer have to pay the £560 tax to the government.

Under this new law, then, neither would be better or worse off than under the existing law. The value of the land when the tax (now paid by the builder) is included is still £1,400. In both cases, therefore, the total outlay required of the builder to secure this piece of land is £1,400. In both cases the net profit secured by the farmer will be £1,400 less £560, or £840.

fact there is always some scope for a little bargaining. This is certainly so. But there is no more scope for bargaining when the government introduces a levy than without a levy. And for the conclusion to be modified it would, indeed, have to be shown that the introduction of the levy affects, in some particular way, the outcome of the bargaining process. It might, of course, be contended that the builder would be willing to pay more just because he knows that the farmer selling him the acre is going to have to pay the levy. But to expect the developer to do so is about as reasonable as expecting him to pay a higher price simply because he learns that the farmer has decided to celebrate the sale by throwing a party at the village pub.

The economist is always ready to admit that if we no longer assume that dealers are trying to make the most money they can from their business transactions, his conclusions no longer hold. It is possible that a farmer will, for sentimental reasons, refuse to sell his land, or refuse to sell it for the largest profit. Unless such behaviour is quite general the economist cannot incorporate it into his economic analysis in order to reach general conclusions. He must, that is, have to hand some theory of generally representative behaviour in business. Up to the present, the theory that people are out to make as much money as they can in business has served the economist pretty well – though obviously it is not the only theory, and not, in every circumstance, the best theory. But no concession need be made here on this score, for those alleging that the levy on land would raise prices did not reach such conclusions by invoking some particular kind of non-commercial behaviour. Quite the contrary; they believed that this result could be reached on the basis of the usual economist's assumption that businessmen seek to maximize their profits.

III

Another possible objection to the orthodox economic conclusion, that the introduction of a levy must leave the price of land unchanged – though not, as it happens, one that was brought forward in this connection – is that the argument ignores the price-expectations of buyers and sellers. If, say, the sellers of land *believe* that the levy will raise the price of land (above that attained in the absence of a levy) then sellers will refuse to sell at the existing (maximum) market prices. If buyers also believe this to be true, they too will be ready to pay higher prices. Apparently 'wishing will make it so' after all.

The economist does not deny that expectations about future price movements influence the course of present prices. The influence of expectations on prices is a well-known phenomenon in organized markets such as the stock exchange or the commodity exchanges. But although such 'false' expectations may, for a while, deflect prices from their equilibrium values, such prices cannot be maintained above their equilibrium for long. In the long run an increase in the market value of land or other assets can be maintained only so long as their future earnings justify the increase in value. This means that if commercial buyers are willing to pay a higher price than that warranted by the eventual market prices of the buildings on this piece of land, they are sure to burn their fingers.

Expectations may enter in a different way, however. Suppose there are political expectations that the levy will be abolished soon, or its rate reduced. The farmer might then refuse to sell his land today. For by waiting until the levy is abolished he will save the £560 he has otherwise to pay to the government. If the developer insists on having the land immediately the farmer will sell provided the developer pays the £560, in addition to his maximum offer of £1,400. But what is sauce for the goose is sauce for the gander. The developer, even if he were not paying the maximum of £1,400, will see no advantage in paying more now if, by waiting, he need only pay a smaller sum. Moreover, the developer would be foolish to pay more than £1,400 for it, as this sum is still the maximum *excess* profit he can make on selling the house. If he pays more, he will be eating into his ordinary ten per cent profit. The correct conclusion then is not that expectations of a reduction or abolition of the levy raise the price of land. Only that the sale of the land would be postponed until the abolition of the levy.

In general, if we expect the levy to be permanent, and if we assume that dealers are inspired only by commercial incentives, such a levy on the capital gains of selling land for 'development' purposes does *not* affect the amount of land sold, and does *not* affect the resultant market price of land. The tax acts only to transfer a part of the gains of landlords to the government.

IV

We may as well touch on a related fallacy before ending: namely, that a cut in building costs will reduce the price of houses. This could happen, but the circumstances under which it will *not* happen are common enough to be worth dwelling upon.

If the amount of building land is strictly controlled by the government and cannot therefore be augmented by agricultural land, there is – subject to density regulations – a most profitable way of building on the existing supply of development land. Let us suppose that prior to a fall in building costs (the result, say, of the invention of a brick-laying machine) the maximum profit that could be made on one acre of such land is by building on it eight type *A* houses, each selling for a price of £3,000: a total house value of £24,000. If the cost of building the eight houses is £14,000, and the price of the acre of land is £6,000, the total cost to the developer is £20,000. He expects a profit of £4,000, or twenty per cent, on his cost. This is the normal profit, let us suppose, in the building trade.

The introduction of the brick-laying machine now reduces the cost of construction of each house by £500, a total reduction in building costs of £4,000 for the eight houses. This augments the builder's profit by £4,000. Building profits are now far above normal, but no more land becomes available on which to build. This does not, however, stop builders competing with one another for the purchase of the existing amount of building land. This competition will bid up the price of the given amount of building land until builders are, once again, left with no more than their normal profit. In our example, so long as building profits are above normal, the bidding and counter-bidding will continue until this one acre has gone up in price by a further £4,000 to reach a total figure of £10,000. However, the normal profits of the builder are the same as before, while the prices of the houses remain unchanged at £3,000 each. The landlord alone benefits from the reduction in building costs.

We must conclude that while the effective amount of building land remains unchanged no reduction of building costs would reduce the price of housing. It would act only to increase the rents of landlords.

Of course, if the government does allow some more agricultural land to be transferred to developers, so increasing the total amount of land available for building, an increased number of houses can now be built. Demand conditions remaining unchanged, the prices fetched by houses will decline. But clearly this result has nothing at all to do with a fall in building costs. Any relaxation of government regulations which causes land to move from agricultural uses to building uses – and the owners of agricultural land will always be glad to transfer it to developers so long as the price per acre for building purposes exceeds that for agricultural use – ultimately augments the supply of housing and, given the conditions of demand, results in a lower price of houses.

Finally, if there were building innovations enabling the developer (in the absence of regulations to the contrary) to build, say, taller buildings than before, the given supply of building land would no longer limit the supply of houses. Given unchanged demand conditions, house prices would have to fall to clear the now greater number of houses put onto the market. This fall in the price of houses would, incidentally, be quite consistent with a rise in the rents of landlords. For builders, again competing with one another, bid up the price of the limited land until the additional profits of constructing taller buildings have been wholly absorbed in rents to the landlord.

5 The National Debt is a Burden

*'The larger is the national debt the greater is the burden to be borne by future generations.'**

In attacking President Kennedy's administration for extravagant spending, ex-President Eisenhower (May 1963) put the case more strongly: 'In effect,' he declared, 'we are stealing from our grandchildren in order to satisfy our desires of today.' Robbing our children is bad enough. Robbing one's grandchildren is unforgivable. Eisenhower's choice of expression evokes a vision of the little tots peacefully asleep while their unprincipled grandpas, reeking of bootleg, furtively pick open the locks of their piggy banks. Less picturesquely, the notion conveyed by such phrases is that improvident living dissipates the inheritance of future generations and acts to impoverish them.

I

First, let us be clear about one thing: that is, that the present generation cannot, in any usual sense, borrow from future generations. International loans are obviously possible. We can add to our current real resources by borrowing from abroad, by using the money lent to us to buy things from abroad and thus add to the goods at our disposal. What we cannot do is add to our goods now by borrowing from the future, for the simple reason that goods to be produced in the future have not yet come into being. If in a fully employed economy, the government proposes to undertake a three-year dam-building programme costing one

*In his State of the Union message (7 January 1960) President Eisenhower said 'Personally I do not feel that any amount [of excess tax receipts over government expenditure] can properly be called a surplus while the nation is in debt. I prefer to think of such an item as a reduction in our children's inherited mortgage.'

billion pounds, and proposes to do this without borrowing from abroad, then, of the aggregate value of goods produced by the country over the next three years, one billion pounds' worth of dam construction will be produced instead of an additional one billion pounds' worth of other goods (both consumption goods and capital goods). In other words, the country as a whole must reduce its expenditure on consumption and other sorts of capital goods together by one billion pounds in order that real resources can be devoted to constructing one billion pounds' worth of dams. No conceivable method of finance – whether the one billion pounds is raised wholly by additional taxes, wholly by government borrowing, wholly by the creation of new money (and therefore by generating inflation), or by a mixture of the three – makes it possible to fulfil this programme without providing the real resources currently. In other words, the real sacrifice of one billion pounds' worth of other expenditure has to be made currently, during the three-year period of the dam-building programme.

We can, of course, transfer things from the present to the future – simply by storing them. But, since time moves in one direction only, we cannot reverse the process and transfer assets which have yet to be produced by future generations into the present. Having affirmed the impossibility of borrowing from the future, let us turn to the possibility of a burden on future generations arising from our borrowing money from ourselves in the present as a nation; or, more specifically, from the government's borrowing from the public – which is what increasing the national debt amounts to.*

II

Let us now imagine that some vast government enterprise, such as the dam-construction programme mentioned, has been successfully financed by the government's borrowing from the

*At least if the government's bonds are all held *within* the country. The usual burden argument, however, does make the simplification that all of the national debt is held by the citizens.

public. For every £100 it borrows the government issues to the lender an interest-bearing £100 bond. Thus, on a certain day each year any person holding such bonds is entitled to receive £5 (or some such sum depending on the interest rate borne by the bonds in question) for each £100 bond. The payment of such annual sums as interest on all the government bonds held by the public is known as 'servicing the national debt'. Year after year, interest payments have to be made by the government to those of its citizens who are bond-holders. If this vast enterprise in question happens *not* to be a 'productive' investment (one that yields, annually, only a pecuniary return) or happens to be insufficiently 'productive', so that the returns are not large enough to meet the annual interest payments on the amount the government borrowed,* then additional taxes have to be raised annually to 'service' the government's debt. But no matter how large the national debt, and no matter, therefore, how large the amount of the interest payments to be met by government taxation, once the debt has been incurred and the money spent there is no further reduction whatsoever in the annual volume of goods and services at the disposal of the community. If, for example, the net national product is £30 billion, the existence of a national debt of either £1 billion or £100 billion cannot alter the fact that the value of the output of goods produced during the year continues to be £30 billion,† and that no part of this is (by assumption) owing to anyone outside the country.

*The word productive is placed in quotation marks to suggest a purely commercial interpretation of the term: the larger the pecuniary return received on the investment the more 'productive' the investment appears. It is, however, quite possible that investments undertaken by governments yield net benefits to the community that are not sold, or cannot be sold, on the market. Such net benefits to the community at large may be capable of calculation and may turn out to exceed the ordinary rate of return on commercial investment. This distinction is of the greatest importance (see Chapter 6) but need not be invoked in the present analysis, at least not for some time.

†It simplifies matters a little to suppose that the country engages in no international trade or that, if it does, its net annual debt to foreigners is nil. The argument which follows does not, however, depend in the least on this simplification.

75

The interest on the internal debt (and even the contribution, if any, to a 'sinking fund'* – by which the national debt can be gradually reduced) will always be paid by one group of people to another group. More precisely the interest on the national debt will be paid by tax-payers as a whole to those particular citizens who hold government bonds. The annual interest payments on the national debt are therefore to be thought of as no more than transfer payments between the citizens of a single country. Irrespective of the size of the debt, these interest payments should be regarded as transfer payments and, therefore, impose no extra burden on the community as a whole, now or in the future.

A small qualification is in order at this stage. It is sometimes believed that a rise in the rates of income tax, which may be necessary to meet additional interest payments, will reduce incentives for people to earn income. At higher tax rates, they may decide to work less. Fewer goods are therefore produced. This is a possibility, although there is no knowledge yet of how far high taxes have to rise before causing people to reduce their incomes and therefore the output of marketable goods and services. The additional tax revenue necessary to pay the interest on the national debt could, of course, be called a 'burden' even though these tax receipts are transferred from the bank accounts of one set of people to those of another set. But it so happens that neither the additional taxation that may be needed to 'service' any (increase in the) national debt, nor the alleged disincentive effects of additional taxation, are the factors that are at issue in the modern concept of the 'burden' of the national debt. This concept of the

*If in any year the government, after meeting all its current expenditures, has more than enough revenue to pay the interest on the national debt, the extra money can be used to pay off some of this debt. The government simply uses the extra money to 'buy back' some of these bonds (through the stock exchange) from the public. It will then owe less to the public, and consequently its annual interest payments will be smaller. Now sometimes, the government will not use this extra money for paying off some of its debts immediately. It will place it for the time being in its account at the Bank of England and earmark it for paying off some part of the debt later. It can then be said to be creating a 'sinking fund'.

'burden' of the national debt is deemed to exist even if the community has no objection whatever to tax-mediated transfer payments, and even in the complete absence of any disincentive effects.

III

If, regardless of the size of the national debt, we allow that whatever the country produces accrues wholly to its inhabitants now and over the future, in what other sense can the national debt be construed as a burden? In fact there have been several attempts to attribute a useful meaning to the 'burden' of the national debt and to indicate the circumstances which would bring it into being. Readers who find this sort of game fascinating may dip into the learned journals for further enjoyment.* There is, however, one concept of the burden of the national debt that has some plausibility about it and, indeed, has had a much wider currency than others. It is worth examining closely for the issues it raises.

This view of the burden turns on the fact that by our economic behaviour today we can add to, or subtract from, the accumulation of capital equipment that will, in the course of time, come to be inherited by future generations. Some rate of accumulation of capital goods – the 'rate of investment' – is always taking place, a large part of it through private investment. If, therefore, the methods of finance used by the government cause us to save and invest less than we otherwise might do, future generations will come to inherit a smaller stock of capital equipment than they would otherwise. And since the stock of capital properly employed yields an annual return or income to its owners, any reduction in the future stock of capital – compared, that is, with what it might have been – entails a smaller income for the future beneficiaries compared with that which they might otherwise have enjoyed.

But how does the government's creation of national debt

* An introduction to the various definitions of the burden of the national debt is to be found in my paper 'How to Make a Burden of the Public Debt', *Journal of Political Economy*, 1963.

reduce capital accumulation? A simple example will provide the essentials of the argument. Let the government in our fully employed economy be faced with the alternatives of raising £1 billion by taxes or by borrowing. If it chooses to raise this sum by borrowing it from the capital market, so increasing the national debt by £1 billion, private capital formation is reduced by this amount. For in a fully employed economy there is, over any period of time, a certain flow of current saving which limits the flow of new investment. If the government attracts to itself £1 billion from this annual flow of saving it leaves that much less saving available for private capital formation. If, on the other hand, this £1 billion were instead raised entirely by additional taxes, the public would have at its disposal £1 billion less. And if, as a result of this £1 billion reduction in their disposable incomes, the public reduced their *consumption* expenditure by exactly £1 billion there would be no reduction at all in the amount of private capital formation. In effect, taxation of an extra £1 billion can be thought of as a form of 'forced saving' that is additional to the normal flow of saving which now remains as before. The government, by raising the £1 billion through additional taxes, extracts an extra £1 billion saving from the public without reducing the flow of saving for private investment.

We can, if we wish, qualify this result a little in the interests of greater realism without in any way weakening the force of the argument. Thus, it is more likely to be the case that a reduction of disposable incomes of £1 billion, as a result of the new taxes, causes people to reduce their consumption expenditure not by the full £1 billion but by some fraction, say four-fifths, of £1 billion. Only four-fifths of this £1 billion is therefore 'forced' saving. The remaining fifth of £1 billion of saving, which is required (in addition to the four-fifths of £1 billion) to offset the government's extra expenditure of a full £1 billion, must then be provided from people's private saving. Private investment – private capital accumulation, that is – has then to be reduced by this fifth of £1 billion.

The upshot is that if the £1 billion is raised by additional taxes, instead of by government borrowing, *private* capital formation is either not reduced at all or else, if we want to be more realistic, it is reduced by only a fraction of the £1 billion. Whereas if instead this sum were borrowed from the public in the ordinary way private capital formation would be reduced by the full £1 billion.* The 'burden' on future generations is, therefore, conceived in terms of a reduction in the size of the capital stock they would have inherited, and therefore of the larger income they would consequently have enjoyed were it not for the government's recourse to borrowing instead of taxation.

IV

Another shaft of light can be directed onto this problem by supposing that the issue now is solely between government borrowing and private borrowing. In this connection there is, in some versions of the 'burden' argument, an additional pre-supposition, not always made explicit, that government expenditure of the sums it borrows, through its issue of bonds to the public, is generally 'wasteful' compared with the use made of borrowed money by private enterprise. Government spending of borrowed money would, for instance, be regarded as 'wasteful' in the relevant sense if such sums were being spent in currently prosecuting a war. There is indeed often a strong bias against government expenditure in general, it being deemed less 'productive' than private expenditure. If, however, the government uses the amounts raised by borrowing for investment in projects that are, always, no less 'productive' than private investment – in that they yield an annual return no smaller than that yielded by investing the same sum in any private investment – the burden argument, as it has been developed so far, does not seem to hold. Future generations will still inherit less *private* capital formation as a result of the government's borrowing. But since the government's borrowing produces capital formation that is no less 'productive', total capital formation – private and public taken together – will be no less than if the government did not borrow at

* Indeed, in so far as the government's borrowing raises interest rates, it may even reduce private capital formation by more than £1 billion.

all, but left all the borrowing and investment to private enterprise. It would seem, then, that the magnitude of this 'burden' on future generations depends on just how the government uses the sums it raises by borrowing. If such sums are spent by the government on assets that are equally as 'productive' as those that are bought by private enterprise – in other words if the government's investments yield as much as the investments undertaken by the private sector – then there appears to be no 'burden'. To the extent the government uses such sums less 'productively', however, there is some 'burden'. If, finally, the government uses such funds more 'productively' than the private sector there is a negative 'burden', or should we say a *benefit*, conferred on future generations.

Before casting a sceptical eye on this sort of reasoning, let us disclose another twist in the argument. It is generally believed by economists that along with the growth in the value of the public's claims to assets there is a decline in its annual saving and, consequently, a decline in the rate of capital accumulation. If government loans are raised in peacetime this alleged fact need not qualify our results. Provided the government uses the funds it raises as 'productively' as the private sector of the economy, the claims of the public have their physical counterpart in real 'productive' assets. And any gradual decline of the annual rate of saving (and, therefore, of the annual rate of capital accumulation) takes place in any case and irrespective of the proportion of government investment in the country's total investment.

Consider now a situation of total war during which there is no private accumulation of capital (except that which is required for war purposes). Indeed there may well be a gradual reduction in the stock of capital. The public's holdings of claims to assets, if they are to reflect the true position, should be reduced to the same extent. If the government, in the prosecution of the war, raises the whole of its vast current expenditure by taxes, then at least we can be sure that by the end of the war the public holds no more claims to assets than it does at the start. If, on the other hand, the government covers a part of this current war expenditure by borrowing from the public, then – although the real sacrifices by the citizen body, in terms of reduced consumption during the war, are just as great as if the sums were raised instead by taxes – the end of the war will find the public holding government bonds that are claims to non-existent assets. For all that, the public regards these bits of government paper as if they were the 'real thing'. So far as the public is concerned, such government war bonds are encashable on the stock exchange and earn interest just like a claim to a 'productive' asset. In consequence of its increased holding of such paper claims, as compared with the beginning of the war, the public's rate of saving and, therefore, the rate of potential capital accumulation, is lower. This annual rate of saving would not, however, have been any lower had the war effort been financed entirely by taxation. For in that case, the public would not have accumulated these bits of government paper that made people feel wealthier by the amounts written on them.* It follows, therefore, that war-time borrowing, in contrast to taxation, acts to reduce the future rate of private capital accumulation. If so, it will also reduce the stock of real assets that will come to be inherited by future generations.

v

The arguments of the last section can be summed up crudely as follows: In so far as government borrowing diverts funds from private investment, and spends these funds on items yielding a rate of return *below* that which could be had on private investment, it imposes a 'burden' on future generations. This 'burden' consists in future generations having a lower real capital stock and, therefore, a lower real income than they might otherwise have enjoyed.

Having presented the reader with the most favourable interpretation of the alleged burden, we must now expose it as a piece of

*As the reader may surmise, the more logical people are the less prone they will be to this 'wealth illusion' in as much as the additional taxes necessary to meet the annual interest payment on the Debt reduces people's income by exactly as much as the bondholders' income is augmented. But since the burden argument is fallacious irrespective of the extent of this 'wealth illusion' we may continue to suppose its existence.

legerdemain rather than a serious economic proposition.

Before turning to this task, however, it may as well be said in passing that even if a person accepted the logic of the burden-proponents without question, he would be hard put to accept the presumed implication: that governments should not borrow from the public – at least not for 'unproductive' purposes. For it is a fact of economic life in the West that the 'real' standard of living per person, at least as conventionally measured, tends to rise continuously over time. It is not too optimistic to expect *per capita* 'real' income in the West to double over the next thirty years. Moreover, as people now recognize, the rise in 'real' standards over time depends very little on the accumulation of capital *per se*. If people saved, net, virtually nothing, so that future generations inherited a stock of 'real' capital no larger than that available to us today, the rise in living standards would continue unabated. As old machinery and plant wore out, they would be replaced by more efficient plant and machinery, and factories and offices would be managed by people having greater technical skills.

The chief factor making for economic growth in modern societies is continuous innovation. So long as sufficient scientific and engineering research continues – and this research is largely institutionalized or 'built into' the economy – real productive power in the economy will continue to grow without any net addition to the stock of capital. Provided only that there is not some entirely unprecedented upsurge of population, living standards may be expected to continue to rise without any addition to the stock of capital. If therefore we did our worst and saved nothing from our incomes, our grandchildren would still be much richer than we are today. This being the case, it is hard to justify a serious concern lest, through government borrowing, our rate of capital accumulation be lower than it might be. Does it matter so much if, by our alleged improvidence today, our grandchildren, and great-grandchildren, turn out to be richer than we are by something slightly less than several-fold? After all, as an irate Congressman once expostulated: 'What has posterity ever done for us?'

The National Debt is a Burden

VI

We are, finally, ready to uncover the pretensions of the 'burden' argument. Let us return, therefore, to our example in which the government raises £1 billion to be spent over three years on a grandiose dam-building programme. If the yield from this investment is expected to be at least as high as that which could be produced by using the £1 billion instead in private investment projects then, in the sense described, there is no 'burden' of the additional £1 billion of national debt. This addition to the capital stock is every bit as good as £1 billion of private capital.

But the inquisitive reader may well be asking himself the question: suppose the government were to raise this £1 billion not by borrowing but by additional taxes instead? Private capital accumulation would then *not* be reduced by this full £1 billion (or by a somewhat smaller figure). In that case public and private capital formation together is greater than it would have been in the absence of the government's initiative. Surely this is better still. Tax finance of a 'productive' investment not merely avoids a 'burden'; it confers a benefit on future generations. Indeed, once our thoughts have broken out in this direction other possibilities appear before us. Why not maintain taxes above receipts continuously and use all the surpluses for 'productive' investment? This will further enlarge the size of the capital endowment to be enjoyed by posterity. Really high taxes which coerced us into austerity would enable us to perform prodigious feats of capital accumulation.

We have goaded the logic of the matter this far in order to make the reader suspect that something is amiss. A sense of symmetry provides the clue. If we are prepared to talk of an additional 'burden' being suffered by future generations whenever we are led to consume some part of current output rather than accumulate it (and thus enable future generations to enjoy a larger stock of capital goods, and so increase their consumption), are we not entitled to talk of a 'burden' being imposed on the *present* generation when, instead, we reduce our consumption in favour of increased consumption by our grandchildren? Alternatively, we might choose to talk of *benefits* rather than of

83

burdens: if we consume more today, as a result of the government's recourse to borrowing rather than to taxation, is there not a 'benefit' enjoyed by the present generation? If we consume less today because of tax finance, can we not talk of the 'benefits' conferred on future generations or, alternatively, the 'burden' imposed on the present generation by resorting to tax finance?

This tentative use of an alternative terminology serves to reveal a real problem. Even if we wished to use such terms as 'benefit' or 'burden' how can we justify them without first agreeing on a norm? Just how much should be saved? The old-fashioned response to such a problem was to regard the rates of interest emerging from a competitive capital market, or a competitive securities' market, as presenting the terms on which the community makes its saving and investment decisions. The existing capital markets are far from being competitive, but even if they were, few economists today would accept that the interest rates resulting therefrom provide a reliable guide to what the community should be saving. Some people believe that political considerations should finally determine the rate of capital accumulation of the community as a whole. Others believe that interest rates should be corrected to allow for interdependence: to allow for the possibility that the amount any person or group is willing to save depends, among other things, on the amounts that all others are willing to save.

We shall not discuss these difficult questions here, for we have said enough to reveal the nature of the real problem that has been concealed by the bogus 'burden' argument. And this real problem turns out to be an *allocative* problem – one of disposing of our resources over time.

The more of our income we consume today, the lower will be the level of the higher consumption of future generations (though, as suggested in the preceding section, the difference it makes is likely to be small). In more general terms, the allocative problem is that of choosing some 'optimal' path of consumption over time. At present, 'real' consumption *per capita* in the West appears to be rising at a certain rate over time. Do we want it to rise more swiftly in the immediate future and more slowly later, or do we want the reverse? or what? Until we have some agreement about the shape of this optimal consumption path over time, we cannot legitimately pronounce any government policy as resulting in too much or too little consumption today or, for that matter, too much or too little consumption tomorrow.

And if economists ever do agree on the characteristics of an optimal consumption path over time they would surely agree also to talk of policies needed to prevent deviations, positive or negative, from that optimal path, rather than adopt politically persuasive terms such as 'burden' that have no rightful place in the vocabulary of economics.

Part 2   Business Fallacies

6 Prices Should Cover Costs

'Only if a good can be sold at a price that covers
its cost should it be produced.'

I

What is the rationale of this commercial criterion? Why should costs be covered? For the businessman the answer is straightforward: if he does not succeed in covering his costs he will not remain long in business. But unless we believe that the purpose of producing goods is to ensure the survival of businessmen we are entitled to press the question; to ask, in fact, how such a criterion serves society?

The question is best answered in connection with a simple example. Suppose the public buys 10,000 cut glass bowls a year at a price per bowl of £1. The £10,000 the public is prepared to pay for them may be regarded as a money measure of their satisfaction with the bowls. Indeed, it is likely to be an underestimate, since some of the purchasers would have been willing to pay more than the price of £1 for a bowl rather than go without. Now look at it from the point of view of costs. If the business is to continue, the £10,000 received must be enough to compensate all those who contribute both to the production and distribution of the bowls – including a reward, profit, for those who lend their money to the firm and bear the risks of the enterprise. But again, the £10,000 that is divided among them is almost certainly more than what is necessary to compensate them exactly for their efforts and sacrifices. For some of them would be prepared to continue making their contributions for something less than the sums they receive for making them.

Apparently then there are net gains on both sides of the market, that is, to both buyers and producers. This can be brought out even more clearly by supposing that the production of these cut glass bowls was prohibited by government decree. Both buyers and producers would then feel they were worse off.

For each buyer would then have to dispose of the pounds he spent on these bowls on alternative goods, which goods he had hitherto rejected in favour of the bowls. As for all those hitherto engaged in producing and marketing the cut glass bowls, they would have to turn to activities which were previously open to them, but which had been rejected so long as the firm offered them those opportunities for gain that have now been withdrawn.

The rationale of the commercial criterion, that price covers cost, emerging from this example appears to be that the production of any good or service is justified if, on balance, there are net gains to the community.

II

But this commercial criterion, as it happens, is neither necessary nor sufficient for an economic activity to result in net gains to the community. Consider these two allegations in turn:

(a) That the commercial criterion is not *necessary*. Certain of the nationalized industries are unable to cover their costs by the sale of their services – the railways for instance – and are subsidized by the government. The justification is that even though they operate at a loss in the commercial sense, the *surplus* of gain enjoyed by the public is more than enough to compensate for this loss. Thus, if a very finely discriminating tariff could be devised – one that was adjusted to extract the maximum payment for each successive unit of good or service from each consumer separately – the total revenue so raised would be more than enough to cover the full costs of the enterprise. And the fact that, for political or administrative reasons, such a tariff cannot be used does not detract from the calculable excess of benefits over costs which, again, justifies the maintenance of the service as one conferring net gains on the community.

It may be noticed in passing, however, that in some cases, such as gas, electricity and the telephone service, a *two-part tariff* is feasible. In such cases a price per unit is set which may not be enough to cover total costs. At this price, however, the consumer buys all he wants. But he is also made to pay a fixed charge for the right to buy any of the good or service at this price. And this fixed charge transfers to the enterprise some of his 'surplus' gain from buying all he wants of the service at the per unit price, thus enabling the enterprise to cover its full costs.

(b) That covering commercial costs is not *sufficient*. The very word commercial draws our attention to items, other than purely commercial costs, which ought to be included in the total costs. By suggesting that any incidental damages inflicted on society at large *ought* to be included in the costs of production we are tacitly making a judgement of fact, that society as a whole would accept the view that the costs of damages inflicted on others are as valid as the commercial costs themselves. One common example of such 'spillover effects' inflicting costs on others is that of a detergent-producing works that starts to pour its effluent into a stream whose waters are used by a distillery. The cost of the damage to the distillery – or the cost of water-purifying equipment required to maintain the quality of its products – should be rightly attributed to the detergent works. And unless the total value of the detergent works' products exceeds the complete *social* costs it incurs – exceeds, that is, both the commercial costs *plus* the minimal cost of the damage inflicted on the distillery – the detergent works should be closed down on the grounds that its operation cannot ensure net gains to the community.

Another popular example is that of the automobile. One might conjecture that by far the greater part of its operating costs is borne not by the owner but by the public at large. Obviously if all the noise created and all the exhaust gases emitted were confined to the interior of the vehicle, the private motorist would choose to adopt other means of locomotion – or else pay for devices that eliminate them. But since he is allowed to throw off these noxious by-products into the surrounding air, to be shared by the population at large, he need never consider his own contribution to the collective din and air-poisoning. For many this is not a minor inconvenience. Those who once took pleasure in strolling through the centre of London or any city, admiring at leisure the historic buildings and landmarks, have been deprived of an enjoyable recreation for which there are no substitutes. Even in suburbs where, in the summer months at least, one could smell the fresh green of the earth, there is now only a depressing odour of fume and dust. These are genuine and heartfelt losses. If the motorists were obliged to compensate us for all such losses (including the loss of life and limb exacted annually) it is doubtful whether many of them could afford this method of transport either for business or pleasure. What is today regarded as a 'necessary' form of transport would become too expensive, and would have to give way to other forms having milder spillover effects.

Another obvious example in this connection is the noise inflicted on the public from commercial aircraft. At present airlines are able – just about – to cover commercial costs alone and show a profit. Under the existing law they may be said to be 'paying their way'. If, however, they were obliged to compensate their 'victims' for the noise inflicted on them, it is more than possible that they would be unable to cover their costs. At present, and in this larger perspective, their operation could be said to inflict net losses on the community. A law which prohibited noise-creation, unless compensation were paid to those whose peace and quiet had been invaded, would not only make commercial airlines almost certainly unprofitable. It would provide them with the strongest possible incentive – the threat of extinction for failure – to engage in technological research to discover really effective noise-muting devices.

III

In contrast to enterprises having adverse spillover effects there are enterprises that have *favourable* spillover effects. Farming is, or used to be, a healthy occupation. If any extension of farming helps to promote the good life, or improves the air we breathe, or in any way confers benefits on society at large, the value of all these non-marketable advantages should be *subtracted* from

92

the commercial costs of farming. Social costs, that is, are here below commercial costs. And provided the sale of their marketable products to the public covers only these social costs (smaller than commercial costs), there will still be a net gain to the community. Put otherwise, farming should be encouraged by paying to farmers a subsidy equal to the extra (non-marketable) benefits they confer on the country at large.

To some extent, the National Health Service may also be justified along these lines. If the prices were set to cover the full market costs of the services provided, the demand for the services would be likely to be substantially smaller than the existing demand for them when, as in Britain, they are provided free.* But the extension of these medical services provides benefits to the community above those enjoyed by the patients themselves, at least in so far as infectious diseases are concerned. The potential value of such benefits conferred on the public at large would then warrant payment of a subsidy of that amount to the National Health Service, a subsidy which should contribute towards lowering the price to the patients of infectious diseases. Whether the subsidy would be of an amount that reduced the price to zero, as at present, is, however, uncertain. No one has yet undertaken a cost-benefit analysis of the National Health Service.

To conclude, it has been shown that covering commercial costs is neither necessary nor sufficient. The conditions under which it would be necessary and sufficient are too tedious to elaborate here. However, the application of what is now popularly known as cost-benefit analysis to many large enterprises, private and public, is no more than a method of taking into account

*True, the community as a whole has to defray the full cost of the service through their contributions and taxes. But then each individual pays a share according to a formula which does not (at present) include the number of his visits to his general practitioner, and which does not therefore depend upon the medical resources he uses during the year. A hundred visits a year will cost him no more than one, or none for that matter. Each additional visit to the doctor is, for all the difference it makes to his disposable income, free and for nothing – a two-part tariff, in effect, with the per unit price set at zero.

'surplus' consumer gains and also the effects of spillovers favourable or adverse. Some enterprises which, under the existing law, appear to be able to pay their way can thus be shown to be entirely uneconomic, or uneconomic unless they contract their output. Other enterprises, such as the railways (or possibly farming) which might otherwise appear unprofitable, or unprofitable unless they reduce production, can thus be shown to be economically viable. A smoothly functioning private enterprise system is not enough.

7 Consumer Choice Rules the Market

*'The fact that a person freely chooses to buy a
good is prima facie evidence that he is better off
with it than without it.'*

I

In a certain sense this can be necessarily true. If a man puts a
pistol to my head and threatens to shoot unless I drink a glassful
of castor oil then I will, if I believe him to be in earnest, gulp it
down without further ado. I may then be said to have chosen to
drink it of my own free will, for it was not forcibly poured down
my throat and I could, of course, have refused to drink it. It
follows also that, in my own estimation, I am better off than if I
had refused to drink the castor oil. For had I chosen not to
drink it I should have been shot dead. One may then legitimately
infer that being alive with a tumblerful of castor oil inside me is,
for me, preferable to being shot through the head.

What must not be inferred, however, is that I positively enjoy
drinking castor oil by the glass.

This extreme example, in which a person's choice is made
under duress, brings out the general point that all choices are
made within limiting circumstances. If I choose to work as a
dustman, it does not follow that I like this work above all other
kinds of work. It may well be that I happen to have no qualification
for other jobs that I like better; that I do not have the financial
resources necessary to train myself for a more pleasant occupation; that if I do not accept this job I shall have to go on unemployment relief, choose a yet more undesirable job, or starve.
Again, if I choose to travel to Broxton by bus, one cannot infer
that I prefer to travel to Broxton by bus rather than by any other
method. I might prefer to travel by train. But there may be no
train service or, if there is a train service, it runs much too late
or the fare is too dear.

In general, one might say that a man makes a choice only
among the alternatives available to him. If the range of alterna-

tives facing him is changed in any particular we can no longer be sure that he will make the same choice. A policy concerned with advancing social welfare cannot therefore confine itself to observing merely the things people choose from among the existing alternatives and providing more of them. It must examine the existing range of opportunities open to the citizen, arising from the activities of private enterprise and the government, with an eye to widening the range of opportunities from which choices are made. Instead of being provided only with additional dustbins to empty, I should prefer an opportunity of borrowing money so as to train myself for a more congenial vocation. Instead of being offered more buses to Broxton, I would be better served by the provision of a better train service or a lower train fare.

In a nutshell, we can depend upon it that people will do the best they can for themselves in the circumstances, no matter how harsh. They will always choose the lesser of two evils, so that their choice is not an infallible guide to their greatest happiness. In particular, the fact that a choice is always made among the existing range of alternatives is no justification whatever for the existing alternatives. One of the tasks of the economist is to make proposals for changing, and extending, the range of alternatives in order to raise the level of satisfaction.

But there are limits to the alternatives that can be produced and there are limits to the terms on which they can be produced. For the economy as a whole, such limits, at any moment of time, are given by the existing technical knowledge and resources – that is to say, by the existing labour force, land, mines, forests, etc., and the plant and machinery, along with the specialized knowledge and skill with which these resources are employed. This allows the community as a whole a choice among the wide range of alternative combinations of goods and services producible by the pool of resources with the existing technology. What combination of goods is ultimately chosen will depend upon the tastes of all consumers in the economy. However, the impact of a man's tastes in determining the combination of goods that are being produced depends upon his income. The larger this is the more weight he carries in determining the outcome. In general then, provided people have different tastes – or provided they buy goods in different proportions at different levels of income – the combination of goods that are produced and sold will depend upon the distribution of income. A shift of purchasing power from rich to poor might, for instance, result in more food and clothing being produced, and less jewellery and Rolls-Royces.

To sum up, *the community's choice is limited by the alternatives that can be made available and by the terms on which they can be made available.* If we use the word 'nature' to summarize the resources and know-how that are available at any moment of time to the community we could say that the community chooses 'on terms presented by nature'. If, for example, the community's tastes change so that it now wants to consume more whisky and less of other things, the ratio between a bottle of whisky and the amount of any one of the other things producible in its stead is given by 'nature'. If, in order to produce 100 more bottles of whisky the (fully employed) economy has to forgo 300 yards of cotton cloth, the 'true' cost of each additional bottle of whisky – 'nature's' terms – is three times that of a yard of cotton cloth. In a highly competitive economy, prices, it is believed, reflect these 'true' costs. If this particular sort of cloth costs 4s. a yard to produce, then a bottle of whisky would cost 12s. If no tax was imposed on either the cloth or the whisky, the bottle of whisky would sell at three times the price of a yard of this cloth. Such prices would faithfully reflect the terms that 'nature' offers. We might then conclude that in the absence of all excise taxes, a highly competitive economy enables people to choose on the terms offered by 'nature'.

II

We now come to the heart of the matter. Under existing legislation the working of the market may be such that the prices do not reveal the terms presented by nature. If the true cost of a ton of steel were £20 and that of aluminium were £60, but, owing to there being a monopoly only in the aluminium industry, its price was set not at £60 but at £110, then other industries' choice between the two metals is guided by misinformation about their relative availability. These other industries would choose less aluminium and more steel than they would if they were faced, instead, with the actual terms on which nature offers the two metals.

And this 'distortion' of 'nature's' terms robs the community, the economy as a whole, of potential gain. For, at the ruling prices, people will be exchanging 110 tons of steel for twenty tons of aluminium, i.e. $5\frac{1}{2}$ tons of steel for each ton of aluminium. If people were allowed to acquire a ton of aluminium by giving up less than $5\frac{1}{2}$ tons of steel they would gain by doing so. In fact 'nature' requires that the economy give up only three tons of steel for one of aluminium. By acquiring more aluminium on these terms, people will be increasing their satisfaction.

Apart from such monopoly practices there are other factors at work to distort the terms on which nature offers us the existing range of goods and services. 'Spillover effects', or the noxious by-products of the operation of certain industries (or of the operations of their products) such as smoke, noise, or pollution, impose costs on the rest of the community but do not enter into commercial costs under the existing law. If a dye factory pours effluent into a stream destroying the fish there, the cost of the fish lost should properly be entered into its costs. If not, the market cost is below the true or 'social' cost. People will then choose to buy more dye at a price below its cost than they would if they had to pay this full social cost – that is, the commercial cost of the dye *plus* the value of the fish that is lost as a result of producing dyes in this way.

Consider another example. In support of plans to accommodate the expanding number of motor-cars a certain professor starts from the premiss that the population is as intent on owning more cars as are the manufacturers in providing them. This, he alleges, is an inescapable fact of economic life. But if the population already owns a stock of fifteen million cars, and apparently chooses to increase its stock of motor-cars by about one million a year, one explanation is that the prices charged for motor-cars are but a fraction of the total costs to society at large. In the first place, there are costs of providing roads and traffic controls, although these may be covered by the road taxes. There are also the costs of using a proportion of our total hospital facilities in tending the victims of motor-car accidents. There are, in addition, the costs of using a large proportion of our police services and of the services of the administration of justice. More important, there are costs that range from mutual traffic strangulation (which can be roughly calculated and charged for) and air pollution to unabating noise and visual disturbance (which are never charged for). There is also the cost to the nation of the people killed each year – running at the rate of 7,000 in Britain, and 53,000 in the U.S. – to say nothing of the toll of those permanently injured, which, in both countries, is many times the corresponding figure for fatalities. Not least is the incalculable cost of the gradual spoiling of the physical environment in which we live. For the motor-car has shaped our environment, and allowed us to spread ourselves further from town and village centres, into an increasingly suburbanized countryside. It has succeeded in creating an environment in which, while it becomes increasingly exhausting to travel it becomes increasingly indispensable to own a private car. It may be difficult to give exact quantitative significance to all of these social costs, yet unless people are made aware of these costs their choices are based on misinformation. In this particular case, the price a person pays for his motor-car is probably a small fraction of the full social costs incurred in its operation.

Furthermore, not only are the *terms* on which the motor-car is made available to the consumer far below its true cost to society, but other *alternatives* that could be made available with society's resources and skill do not emerge from the market under the existing law. For instance, for a sum that is a small part of the nation's total expenditure on maintaining private cars and all the services accessory to their upkeep, it would be possible to provide a comfortable, efficient and frequent public transport service (bus, train, or, wherever practicable, subway) covering all the major population centres in the country, urban and suburban. Such a programme is the pre-requisite to over-coming the growing apathy and 'slumification' of our built-up areas – and the pre-requisite, therefore, to the success of any attempt to restore the charm of our historic towns and villages, and to restore the dignity and sense of community in our cities.

III

Let us sum up.

It is wholly unsatisfactory to justify the existing goods being produced by the economy on the grounds that people have shown by their choices that this is what they want. For what they choose freely to buy depends on what is offered to them and on the prices charged. And, as we have indicated above, neither the full range of feasible opportunities nor the proper costing of existing goods and services can be assumed to emerge from the operation of competitive markets alone. Government initiative has a decisive role to play. By legislating against a variety of discommoding spillover effects, in particular against unwanted noise and pollution of air and water, the government not only promotes equity. It causes the prices of many goods and services to be revised upwards so as to allow for social costs, thereby correcting the information on which the community bases its choices. Again, by setting up agencies charged with the planning of a variety of quiet zones, free from air traffic and private cars, the government makes available to men vital choices of environ-ment that the market does not offer. These and many other opportunities which could add immensely to the satisfaction of many citizens are unlikely to émerge from the profit-seeking activities of private enterprise under existing laws, but must wait on government initiative – or on legislation prompted by the public's initiative.

8 Business Should Be Left to Businessmen

'If it is good for business it is good for the country.'

I

As a matter of historical fact there has never been an economy operated solely by uninhibited private enterprise. The doctrine of *laissez faire*, as understood by economists, always reserved certain areas of enterprise to the state – defence and administration, enforcement of contracts, protection of people and property, and control of the money supply. The claims made on behalf of the system of *laissez faire* were attractive; that operating within the legal framework, the pursuit of private interest would be led 'by an invisible hand' to promote the public good. Today it is recognized among economists that, besides the existence of a legal framework, a number of other conditions must be met before the working of the invisible hand can be depended upon. It is also recognized that these conditions are less likely to be met today than they were at the time Adam Smith was writing – in the second half of the eighteenth century. The only reliable feature today of the private enterprise system is that it operates more efficiently than does a centrally planned economy in preventing prolonged shortages: there is less queueing in America than in Russia. If people want more of a good at a price which covers its cost of production, the additional supply will be forthcoming sooner under private enterprise, unless governments somehow intervene. This relatively rapid response of supply to effective demand is an advantage we can learn to appreciate only by living in a country, or through a period, in which it is inoperative. Nonetheless, there is a good deal more to promoting the public interest than preventing the formation of queues.

One fact the reader must always bear in mind when discussing business questions: Adam Smith's conception of private enter-

101

prise (no different from that of the Utilitarian economists of the nineteenth century, nor from that of economists today) was that of a *means* to a desired end. Business activity was not, and is not, to be regarded as an end in itself. True, from time to time the freedom to engage in profitable enterprise has been represented as an essential freedom by business spokesmen, especially in the United States. But this view of private enterprise, as a vital freedom in its own right and irrespective of its consequences on society, can count on no support from political philosophers or political economists. Where it is defended by them, it is defended solely as a means to desirable public ends. The two most popular arguments in favour of private enterprise are (*a*) that (provided the economy is fairly competitive) it disperses economic power and acts as a counterweight to the powers of the state, and (*b*) that it is an inexpensive way of producing and distributing the individual goods used in the economy, and of rewarding people for the economic services they perform.

From these introductory remarks we may appreciate the so-called presumption in favour of private enterprise (for the two reasons given above) while recognizing that the ends pursued by business need not necessarily coincide with the public interest.

Business activity is used ambiguously in the dictum heading this chapter. In order to examine the allegation that what is good for business is also good for the country we shall distinguish between the level of business or economic activity as a whole (in II), and the activities of particular units of business, either industries or firms (in III).

II

We may begin by agreeing that a higher level of overall economic activity, as indicated by a higher level of employment in the country, is generally to be preferred to a lower one – provided, always, that inflation is kept under control. Businessmen and the public at large would concur in preferring a higher level of employment, which concurrence offers about as much concession to the allegation in question as can be offered. And it is not really very much. For it suggests neither that the purpose of maintaining a high level of economic activity in the country is the strengthening of private enterprise, nor that private enterprise, in pursuit of its own interest, is able deliberately to create the high level of economic activity and employment which is preferred by the country as a whole. The first point is obvious enough so let us turn to the second.

Not so very long ago, there lived a happy doctrine which said that 'supply creates its own demand'.* It was as if a businessman, observing idle labourers about the vicinity, were to set up a shoe factory. By paying out incomes to the labourers, and setting a price which gave a profit to himself, there should be enough purchasing power created to buy up the output of shoes. But from this simple arithmetical proposition one cannot infer that the new shoe output will be bought. The newly employed labourers might want to spend only a small proportion of their income on shoes. If this example does not seem quite fair, we can suppose, instead, a much larger number of hitherto idle labourers being taken into employment by many firms all producing different sorts of goods. To make the result more plausible still we can further suppose that the additional items provide all the goods that will be required by the newly employed men. In these circumstances it might, at first, seem that business enterprise, in pursuit of profit, is indeed able to benefit itself and the public. But, as it turns out, employment created in this way cannot be maintained. There are, in the complex economies of today, certain institutional facts which prevent employment being increased in this apparently straightforward way. Supply can no longer be depended upon to create its own demand. Why not?

Suppose there are one million unemployed men. If they spread themselves among the existing factories, their new employment would produce, let us say, additional output worth £1 billion a

*The doctrine is chiefly associated with the French economist J. B. Say. In particular see his *Traité d'économie politique* (8th edition, Paris, 1876), especially pp. 150–51.

year. Now if, at the same time, an additional *demand* of £1 billion a year were created for the products of industry, all would be well. Of course, even if there were this additional £1 billion-worth of demand, it might be for a collection of goods somewhat different from the actual assortment being produced. In that case industry would have to switch its capacity to producing less of some goods and more of others, so as to give the public exactly the assortment it wanted. But this task of shifting employment between industries so as to adapt an existing productive capacity to the wants of consumers is a continuous one. We can ignore it here in order to compare aggregates – that is to say, to compare the value of the additional total demand newly generated with the addition to the value of total output.

Now it is a well-established fact that out of every additional £1 of income received less than £1 will be spent on domestic goods by the recipients. The fraction of this pound that is not spent on domestic goods is saved, and/or spent on imports, and/or paid in taxes. If on the average say only three-quarters of each additional pound of income were spent on personal consumption goods, then an additional £1 billion of incomes (earned in producing the additional £1 billion of output) would generate an additional domestic demand of only £750 million. It follows that of the additional £1 billion of output produced, there would be £250 million-worth left unsold at the end of the year. As stocks accumulate firms will begin to realize that they are producing more than the public wants to buy. They will then reduce supplies by laying off workers. But even if they reduced the additional output to half the previous figure, that is to £500 million, only three-quarters of £500 million, or £375 million, would be bought, and so on. Indeed, only when nothing additional was produced, and the one million men were all out of employment again, would equilibrium be restored and the firms able to sell all they produced.

Put this way, the situation looks very grim. How do we, then, bring these unemployed men back into industry? If, in the above example, the government were to reduce taxation so that the public as a whole spent £250 million more, then this sum plus the £750 million of new demand generated from the additional £1 billion of income, would add to a total of £1 billion of new demand. Additional demand would then be exactly equal to the value of additional output, and all would be well. As an alternative to reducing taxes the government could undertake a programme of public spending large enough to create the required additional £250 million demand for the products of industry. Yet again, the government could have intervened in the 'money market' so as to reduce interest rates and make borrowing easier for private firms. If private firms could thereby be induced to spend £250 million on new plant and machinery, this demand would take up the remaining quarter of the additional one million men employed, producing the £1 billion of output. There are, then, several ways in which the government could increase aggregate demand if there were unemployment of men and machines. And obviously it would not have to wait on any initiative by industry before it engaged in any of these measures.

It should be apparent therefore that in the absence of government intervention – either in the money market or through changes in taxation or government expenditures – the economy may be unable to maintain a satisfactory level of employment. The total demand for domestic consumption goods generated by the incomes created in the full employment of our productive capacity will always be less than the value of output produced (being only three-quarters of it in our example). Unless this resulting deficiency in aggregate consumer demand is made good by some additional demand for industrial plant and machinery – by private investment in fact – the full capacity level of employment cannot be maintained without government intervention.

Under existing institutions the demand for private investment needed to make up aggregate demand to a total equal in value to full capacity output (or to very close to full capacity output) does not come about automatically. The government has to intervene. Where it does not intervene, or does not intervene with sufficiently radical measures, there can be prolonged and widespread unemployment, as there was during the inter-war period. The opposite danger needs no emphasis in the post-

105

war period. An excess of aggregate demand today is as chronic as a deficiency of aggregate demand was before the war. What is no longer in question, however, is the government's clear responsibility for ensuring a high level of economic activity along with price stability.

We may note in passing, however, that a high level of employment, or 'economic activity', is consistent with an unlimited variety of outputs. Indeed, with the passage of time, changing tastes and changing technology require the expansion of some industries and the contraction of others: capital and employment thus shift over time from industry to industry. No one industry is required to be of any particular size. It prospers or declines according as the public favours its products or tires of them, or according as the government subsidizes its products or taxes them. These continuing adjustments in the size of the various industries are not expected to have any but transitional effects on the level of activity as a whole.

The conclusions of the preceding discussion may be summarized as follows. It may be in the interests of business to increase private investment which, in the absence of effective and timely intervention by the government, could create a dangerous inflation. On the other hand, it may appear to be in the interests of business to cut back investment plans which, again in the absence of government intervention, could result in large-scale unemployment. What is good for business in the case of 'too much' private investment, or what appears to be good for business in the case of 'too little' investment, does not obviously coincide with the interests of the public at large. The institutional framework then is not enough: the government must ever be vigilant in its role as regulator of aggregate demand in the economy.

III

We now move on to examine the thesis that what is good for business is good for the country with respect to *particular* industries or firms.

The penultimate paragraph of the preceding section suggests that the claims of businessmen with regard to the benefits conferred on the community by virtue of the value of output they produce in the aggregate, and the employment they provide, are vacuous. It suggests also that no particular firm is needed to provide employment for any given number of people.

'Our works in North Braggshire employs 17,000 men,' says the chairman in his protest to a government plan to place a tax on the industry. The impression conveyed is that all, or most, of these 17,000 men would be thrown out of employment if the demand for the firm's products were reduced as a result of the tax. Whereas – allowing, for the moment, that the workers were as content to be employed in one firm or industry as another – discharged workers will be able to find employment elsewhere so long as the government discharges its responsibility for maintaining the aggregate level of demand and employment.* Indeed, in the high employment economy of today, the burden should be on the employer of labour to justify his appropriation of so large an amount of the limited labour supply.

True, it takes time and expense to change from one firm to another, and more time and expense still to change from one sort of job to another. Workers may not be indifferent as between working in the existing firm and working in a different firm or industry or occupation. They may prefer to live in North Braggshire rather than, say, in South Blimpton. And if the government's action is going to result in the closing down of some of the North Braggshire factories, these considerations must enter into its calculations. It must also take into account the possibility that some of the displaced personnel – like some of the older Welsh miners – are unsuited to other kinds of work. Far from producing as much, or greater, value elsewhere, they will contribute nothing at all to the national output if they are discharged from their industry.

Thus, if the chairman contended that the re-allocation of

---

*And if the government fails to discharge its responsibility there will be unemployment in the aggregate whether this particular firm is affected or not.

resources entailed by the government's scheme imposed a particular hardship on a number of the firm's employees, or put them to unjustifiable expense, the facts could be checked and the government scheme modified in the light of the findings. But such a contention is very different from the original announcement of the chairman which seemed to suggest that the firm found work for 17,000 perople many of whom could not again be gainfully employed if the firm were made to contract its output.

'If it's good for General Motors, it's good for the country' runs the proud slogan, and for no better reason than that firm employs a great many people. But if all the General Motors factories were blown to bits overnight, the remaining motor-car firms would be only too glad to expand their existing capacity and take over the temporarily unemployed automobile workers. Indeed, if the government decided that automobile output should be halved, or abolished, the consuming public would perforce direct its expenditure to other goods, the production of which would then require additional labour. Apart from the unavoidable transitional effects whenever there is a switch in consumer demand from one group of goods to another, whether spontaneous or induced, no long-term alteration in the aggregate level of employment is called for.

IV

So far we have been saying that the size of the firm or industry, though obviously important for the shareholders and management, is of no special concern to the public in so far as the overall level of employment is at issue. But the size of the firm, or at any rate the size of the industry, may be of public concern for another reason – the production by industry as a whole of an 'ideal' assortment of goods. This is not merely a matter of industry providing goods that people are ready to pay for at prices that cover their corresponding costs. If this were all, our chairman would be strongly advised to abandon the threat-of-unemployment story and appeal instead to the potential frustration of the public. The public, he could argue, is being compelled by government intervention to forgo purchases of goods they want, at prices which cover their costs of production, and to redirect their purchasing power into less preferred channels.

However, it is not self-evident that it is in the public interest to produce everything that people are ready to buy at a price which covers cost.* It would, for example, be highly beneficial to private enterprise to produce and sell fire-arms to any person willing to pay for them. Tobacco manufacturers could make greater profits if they were allowed to produce miniature cigarettes, with peppermint flavour, for children. A licence to sell hallucinatory drugs to the public would be worth millions to any drug manufacturer. Yet the existing consensus in Western countries is that the uninhibited manufacture and sale of such things is contrary to the interests of the public.

Such examples may serve also to remind us that the dividing line between 'good' goods and 'bad' goods cannot always be clearly drawn. But the uncertainty as to where the line should be drawn at any time does not weaken the general argument. One has to recognize only that some goods are, or may be, on the wrong side of the line to perceive that what is profitable for business need not promote the public welfare.

Apart from such examples, there is a growing category of goods which, while having obvious utility for their buyers, are invariably a nuisance to others.† They are profitable to industry but not unambiguously beneficial to the public. The public benefit might increase if the output of such products were reduced, or their use made subject to controls, or in some cases forbidden. I am referring here to adverse 'spillover effects', such as unwanted noise, fume, stench, lake and stream effluent, air pollution and the destruction of natural beauty and wild life.‡ These undesirable by-products of modern hardware are clearly not in the public interest, yet they are produced along with

* See also Chapter 6.

† Alternatively, the *process* of manufacturing the product may have unwanted effects on others.

‡ See also Chapters 7 and 21.

the benefits. There is, in principle at least, no unsolvable problem here. The right assortment of goods would tend to be produced in a competitive private enterprise economy if a law were enacted that gave manufacturers the option either of incurring expenditures necessary to the removal of any offensive features arising in the production or use of their products, or else (while research into these possibilities was being undertaken) of fully compensating those adversely affected by the production or operation of the products in question. Once institutions were developed so as to give effect to such a law the burden of curbing these social costs would be borne by those responsible for generating them in the first place, and not, as at present, borne by the rest of the public.*

V

Finally there are other things that are undoubtedly very good for business as a whole, but which may be injurious to the rest of the country. Business as a whole would, if they thought they could get away with it, gladly import unlimited supplies of cheap labour from abroad. But the newcomers, once they entered the country in large numbers, could hardly expect a welcome from the indigenous working population. Whatever the 'optimal' size of the population – if there is such a thing – businessmen will always favour a larger population than the existing one simply because they favour expanding markets in which to sell their wares. Property-owners, and particularly land-owners, also stand to gain from an expanding market, especially in a country

*It is commonly believed that if, instead, the victims of spillover effects came together in order to bribe the manufacturers to curb their spillover-creating outputs the economy would also tend to approach an ideal allocation. This would be roughly true, however, only if the costs associated with the initiative and organization necessary to make such an approach were clearly below the worth of the benefits that could be anticipated by the victims – which is highly unlikely for all significant spillover effects. (The reader interested in the difference made to the resulting allocation by a change in the law respecting compensation will find the arguments developed in Chapters 5 and 6 of my *Costs of Economic Growth*.)

such as Britain where land is scarce relative to population and where, therefore, land and site values in towns and cities would be sure to rise in terms of other goods.

On the population question, therefore, the interests of businessmen and of rentiers are opposed to the interests of the working population and, to some extent also, of the professional groups. The more rapidly population increases – whether solely from the natural growth of the indigenous population or partly also from a net inflow of migrant population – the greater is the tendency for rents and profits to rise at the expense of wages. More important still for countries with high population densities, such as Britain, there is a strong presumption that additional population will subtract from, rather than add to, the existing state of amenity.*

This last statement has application *within* countries also. Counties and municipalities advertise widely not only to attract tourists but to attract commerce and industry into the area. The local authorities stand to gain from the rise in tax revenues. Existing land-owners benefit from the additional demand for land, and existing property-owners in the towns stand to gain from the upward pressure on site values. In the meanwhile, and until site rents are revised upwards, shopkeepers and hoteliers will also enjoy profits from increased sales and custom.

Such gains, however, do not represent a benefit for the country as a whole. For the country as a whole it is true that the gradual growth of industry and population will cause land and site values in general to rise over time. But within this total effect the local movements of population and industry represent no more than a transfer of income and wealth from one part of the country to another. Sites become scarcer, and therefore tend to rise in value, in the towns and cities *towards* which industry and population are moving; they become less scarce and therefore tend to decline in value in the towns and cities *from* which industry and population are moving. The interests of the municipal and county authorities, the interests of landlords and property-owners, are here directly in conflict with those of the

* See Chapter 15.

citizens. For the continued movement of population, industry and commerce, that settles within and around already large and congested urban centres such as London, Birmingham, Liverpool, Oxford, Bradford, Wolverhampton, adds further to the traffic congestion there, and to the noise, fume, filth and – given current building standards – to an ugly and dehumanized environment.

Indeed, for some time now, the government – in tacit recognition that what is good for business is *not* always good for the country – has been taking counter-measures to discourage industry and population from moving into the South-East, and especially from moving into the London area. Inducements are provided to private firms to set up factories in the depressed ('development') areas, though with only limited success up to the present.

9 Expenditure on Commercial Advertising is Warranted

*'The distinction between persuasive advertising
and informative advertising cannot be maintained.
Advertising must therefore be accepted as a
means of providing information.'*

Indeed, some writers have gone so far as to argue that the distinction between persuasion and information is 'fundamentally meaningless'. And though this may look like a species of verbal quibble, the allegation serves to conceal a crucial issue.

I

Let us begin, however, by affirming that there is a distinction between these two terms, as anyone can discover for himself by recourse to a dictionary. We might agree, then, that *information* consists of statements that purport to be true, and pertinent to the answers sought; and that *persuasion* is the process of influencing the opinions of others, generally by means of argument and information – though the use of suggestion, or sheer fantasy, is not excluded either.

Let us succumb to the temptation to invoke statements that seem at first wholly one or the other. Consider the following:

(*a*) 'My Uncle Septimus passed away on 15 October 1957.'
(*b*) 'The Black Box Musigram weighs 7½ lb., measures 10 ins. by 6 ins. by 2 ins., has long, medium, short and V.H.F. wavebands, an extendible aerial, twenty-one transistors . . . and costs £19 19s. 11d. (including tax).'
(*c*) 'Every third smoker smokes Nicotinas.'
(*d*) 'Lisrep washes whiter.'
(*e*) 'He prefers his companions beautiful, his interests exciting – and his coffee laced with Boozup pure Irish whiskey.'

Certainly (*a*) looks like information, but the quibbler would argue that such a notice is an attempt to elicit sympathy, and therefore has persuasive undertones. (*b*) looks like a straightforward description of the facts concerning the appearance and capacity of the Musigram. But facts may speak eloquently. As for (*c*), it may well be a fact that every third smoker smokes Nicotinas. But notifying people of this fact is designed to persuade them to change to Nicotinas by suggesting that their popularity be accepted as an index of their excellence. The statement that 'Lisrep washes whiter', though plainly indicating that Lisrep is a washing agent, is strictly speaking a non-statement until we are told just what it washes whiter than – notwithstanding which it is obviously intended to convey the notion that Lisrep washes whiter than any other washing agent.

Persuasion through suggestion is the dominant element in (*e*). There may indeed be an occasional immaculately attired self-possessed executive in the waiting-room of an airport, the cynosure of all eyes, who combines this extraordinary preference for beautiful women and 'exciting interests' with a taste for coffee laced with Boozup whiskey. But the advertiser does not have to meet one before depicting him. Indeed our logic-chopper will point out that one cannot exclude the possibility of there being such men; and that the more successful is the advertisement the greater are the chances of the story becoming true.

So what are we to conclude? We might conclude, tentatively, that some advertisements are more clearly persuasive than others. Likewise, some advertisements are more clearly factual than others. However, this conclusion might suggest that the distinction between persuasion and information is rather like the distinction between, say, life and death, in that it is occasionally difficult to draw the line – notwithstanding which the distinction is valid and useful. But terms like 'persuasion' and 'information', unlike the terms 'life' and 'death', do not belong to the opposite ends of a spectrum in between which there are intermediate gradations. The terms information and persuasion, even in their 'purest' form, are not necessarily opposed in meaning. The persuasive potential of an advertisement, for

example, may well be increased with the amount of information
provided.

II

Apparently the choice of such categories as persuasion and
information in relation to advertising is something of a red
herring. For it suggests, first, that they are opposing attributes,
and, secondly, that the determination of whether an advertisement falls into the one category or the other is the critical issue.
One has then only to show that in most advertisements the two
are combined to confound the investigation before it gets
started. However, this is *not* the critical issue. It might be if the
case against advertising were that it did not provide information,
or that it provided misinformation, or too little information and
too much persuasion. And it would be, if it were ever proposed
to set up an official body to vet each and every advertisement on
the basis of this distinction and, perhaps, to approve the informative advertisement while rejecting the persuasive one.

But the case against advertising must be made, as against any
other practice and institution, on grounds of uneconomic use of
resources in meeting socially desirable ends. Provided we believe
that the provision of information to the public – in order to
enable it to make more satisfactory choices among the variety
of goods offered to it by modern industry – is a desirable social
end, then the critical distinction is not that between persuasion
and information but between *partial* information and *impartial*
information.

The advertiser is not concerned primarily with providing
impartial information: he would not be in business long if he
were. He is concerned wholly with increasing the sales of the
products advertised. If the statements he makes happen to be
true, this is incidental to his task. I am not suggesting that
advertisers are wholly unscrupulous or irresponsible. They may
well abide by a reasonable code of ethics. But the fact remains
that, in virtue of his vocation, the advertiser cannot be concerned with the whole truth (so far as it may be discovered):

115

only with that part of it that would appear to promote the sale of the advertised goods.

The aim of an agency entrusted with the provision of impartial information, on the other hand, is to provide 'the whole truth' – in the sense of providing 'complete' and 'relevant' information on the basis of objective tests* of rival products. That the results of these tests, when announced, may be deemed persuasive is irrelevant in this connection. What is relevant is that the investigation be undertaken in a scientific spirit and free, therefore, from any intended bias.

In order to avoid misunderstanding let us say something about the two words above in quotation marks. By 'relevant' I mean any information that enters into the consumer's decision. If he thinks that looking like, or acting like, other people is impor- tant, then information on the proportion of people using, or likely to be using, some article or service becomes relevant. By 'complete' I mean *all* information that is relevant. Clearly, com- pleteness must be regarded as an aim, the more of it at a given cost the better. But one has always to limit the investigation by the resources at one's disposal: consumer research organizations of necessity must limit the choice of goods, and the choice of characteristics that are tested, over a given period of time by

*An objective test is one carried out under the strictly standardized conditions required by good statistical method. The conditions of the test are reported so that anyone willing to go to the expense may repeat the test.

We should note in passing, however, that certain relevant characteristics of goods, such as taste, tone, appearance, present more difficulties than such things as weight, volume, strength, efficiency, and so on. The usual procedure for the former range of characteristics is to have a panel of laymen, or experts, agree on the ordering of rival products on the basis of any single characteristic, say fidelity of tone. Such tests, though more directly based on subjective judgement, are 'objective' only in the possibility of being able to repeat them. The more the results of such repeated experi- ments tally, the greater is the degree of confidence which may be reposed in the likelihood of any future test of this sort giving the same result.

If such a method is not completely satisfactory, there is no other method that is. What matters is that most people would prefer to have panel judgements for the subjective qualities of rival products than to have no guidance at all, or to have merely the biased opinions of advertisers.

reference to their finances and the technical facilities available to them. It is not, therefore, very much to the purpose to argue that coverage was limited or that certain tests were inadequate. For these alleged defects can be attributed to a lack of resources or a lack of efficiency which, in the course of time, may be over-come. What is to the purpose is that such an organization operates on an entirely different principle from that of the advertiser. The aim of the advertiser is to promote sales: any information pro-vided by the advertiser is selected almost entirely to serve that end. The aim of the consumer research service, on the other hand, is to provide only impartial information to the consumer.

Provided one accepts as a desirable social end the provision of impartial, and ever more complete, information* to the public, there does not appear to be much one can say in favour of continuing to use the present methods of advertising rather than directing the same amount of resources into the provision of consumer research organizations. However, not everyone is convinced of the desirability of providing impartial information.

III

Objections to the establishing of impartial information services are not to be taken very seriously.

We make brief mention of three:

(a) The standard objections against any extension of the state 'bureaucracy'. Whether such a service should be owned or operated by the state or by private interests, or a mixture of the two, can be settled by reference to pragmatic rather than dog-matic considerations. As it happens, successful consumer information services, both here and in America, were started by private enterprise. But where such a service does not exist, or

---

*Such information should also comprehend a brief description of new products coming onto the market prior to their being tested. The claims of the manufacturer could also be summarized, though obviously without the consumer research organization taking on any responsibility for the veracity of such claims. Information about sales – what, when and where, much like that provided by *Daltons* or *Exchange and Mart* – would also form a desirable supplement to consumer information.

117

where it exists but is inadequate or inefficiently run, there is no strong case against state initiative or intervention.

(b) The argument that the public has given no indication that it wants such a service is not impressive.* If it were taken seriously it would be hard for businessmen to justify their continued innovations in products and services. So far as I am aware there was no public clamour for railways before they were invented, nor for telephones, nor for zip fasteners. The service in question should be offered to the public over a period of time. If the demand falls short of that necessary to support the service, we can investigate further. As it happens, however, existing consumer research services are already self-financing.† The more interesting question is therefore how far they might usefully be extended.

(c) The allegation that a lot of the information provided by such an organization would be either of limited interest or too technical is insubstantial. True, some information about, say, chocolate bars, or sixpenny ball-point pens, may hardly be worth gathering. Such items use up too small a proportion of a person's expenditure for it to matter much if he buys an inferior product. Moreover, the variation in quality between the best and the worst may contribute too little to his total satisfaction to be worth any prolonged investigation. Which items the public is interested in and which not, and the degree of technical information that is desirable, are themselves subjects of investigation.‡ To some extent the answers to such questions could be discovered over time by setting up a centralized service prepared, at a price that covers cost, to furnish the specific information wanted by any single consumer. There are many ways in which such a service could operate. It could, for example, be incorporated into the existing telephone service.

* _Which?_ magazine in Britain claims about two million readers.

† _Which?_ magazine covers its full costs without subsidies and, incidentally, without accepting any commercial advertisements. But even if it were unable to cover its costs, bearing in mind that many benefit who do not subscribe, it may be economically justified (see Chapter 6).

‡ _Which?_ magazine circulates a questionnaire among its subscribers to discover which products they would most like to be investigated.

IV

Turning now to the more radical proposal that would abolish the existing system of commercial advertising, we encounter four* main objections. They are: (a) that advertising subsidizes newspapers (and television services), (b) that advertising also provides entertainment, as a sort of joint product, (c) that people prefer partial information to impartial information, and (d) that the abolition of advertising would amount to a denial of free speech and an infringement of individual liberty.

(a) If a motor-cycle manufacturer paid a newspaper a sum equal to that which would *exactly* defray costs to the newspaper of displaying his advertisement, there would, obviously, be no 'surplus' revenue to the newspaper which could then be passed on to the public in the form of a reduction in the price of the paper. But, as a rule, the manufacturer will pay more money for the advertisement than that necessary to cover the full costs of labour and materials used to reproduce it. This extra money (above the full costs of the advert) can be regarded as a 'transfer

*I doubt whether advertising men still continue to claim that by promoting the sales of a product the economies of large-scale production are realized and passed on to the public. Economists, at any rate, take up the reverse position: competitive advertising, just because it maintains the sales of scores of slightly differentiated products, allows the volume produced of each specific type to be so small that for each the technical advantages of large-scale production has to be forgone. Each firm producing, say, a slightly different kind of soft drink can then legitimately claim to be producing a volume of output at which unit cost falls as output increases. Yet only in so far as the advertising campaign of one or another of such firms is successful enough to break up the existing equilibrium, and to promote the sales of its products at the expense of those of other firms, is it able to avail itself of the economies of large-scale production. However, in the absence of this sort of competitive advertising, direct price competition between such firms would tend to eliminate any that did not eventually expand output to avail itself fully of the technological advantages of large-scale production. In other words, the substitution of price competition rather than advertising competition between firms would act to reduce the number of firms, increase the volume of output produced by each, and continue to do so until unit costs could not be lowered further. (See also the third paragraph of Chapter 13, Section I.)

Twenty-one Popular Economic Fallacies

payment', from the manufacturer to the newspaper readers, via the newspaper-owners. But the motor-cycle manufacturer has to cover his full costs to survive; to cover, that is, both *production* costs and *selling* costs. The price of the motor-cycle must therefore include the advertising costs as well as the production costs. On the other hand, the revenue received from the sale of newspapers is *less* than the total costs of their production, the difference being made up by the 'transfer payment' received from the motor-cycle manufacturer.* The price of these motor-cycles is therefore above their full production costs while the price of newspapers is below their full costs of production. The buyers of motor-cycles are, in effect, subsidizing the newspaper customers (in addition to covering the real costs of the advertisement). Most economists would classify this economic arrangement as a subsidy to newspapers. However, we do not need to argue about the use of terms, only about the economic consequences of this method of finance.

There is both a 'distributional' effect and an 'allocation' effect. The distribution effect in this case means nothing more than a shift of 'real' income from motor-cycle users to newspaper readers: members of the former group pay more than the real costs incurred in making motor-bikes, as a result of which members of the latter group pay less than the real costs incurred in producing newspapers.† As for the allocation effect, this arises from prices being set above the total costs (even above total costs which include the real cost of advertising) of making motor-cycles, and below costs in producing newspapers. Now there may be good economic reasons why newspapers should be sold below costs and why motor-cycles should be priced above costs.‡ But this effective tax on motor-cycles, and subsidy on

* For simplicity I am assuming newspapers do not make more than 'normal' profits (i.e. a normal return on their initial capital). It is, of course, quite possible for newspaper-owners to make abnormally large profits and yet, because of net advertising revenue, lower the price of their newspapers below their costs of production.

† Clearly there can be people who are members of *both* groups; i.e. who are motor-cyclists and readers of this particular newspaper.

‡ See Chapter 6.

120

newspapers, would be just what is wanted only by sheer coincidence. Moreover, this tax-subsidy effect, in some degree or other, arises in connection with all advertised products. Until there are acceptable economic reasons for believing that all newspapers confer benefits on the community which so exceed in value the real costs of producing newspapers as to warrant the existing subsidies – and also, therefore, an extension of their sales at the lower (subsidized) price – there is no presumption in favour of their present subsidy at the expense of other goods.*

(b) True, some advertisements do provide entertainment, or attempt to do so. But advertising and entertainment are not inseparable products ('joint products') any more so than are newspapers and newspaper advertisements. One can, without too sustained an effort of imagination, visualize a newspaper without any advertisements, and also an advertisement without a newspaper. The advertisement could be offered to the public as a leaflet or brochure free, or at a price that covers its cost. Obviously the advertisement need not attempt to provide entertainment.

Is there any reason why advertising, which piques itself on being a service to the public, should not be sold at a price which covers its costs? No apparent reason presents itself. Advertisers may reasonably suspect that if they sold pure advertisements by the yard to the public at a price set to cover costs, they would sell

---

*Advertisers like to believe that advertising is a source of support to a free Press. But the use of newspapers as a medium of advertising can have at least one socially undesirable consequence – that of reducing the number of independent newspapers.

It is occasionally alleged that only newspapers with a really large circulation can reap the economies of large-scale production. But even if there were zero economies of scale – say, the per unit production costs of 10,000 copies were no different from those of 1,000,000 or more – there can be large financial advantages of size if advertising charges increase sufficiently with circulation. Defining as a subsidy the excess charge to the advertiser over the full costs of the advertisement to the newspaper, the estimated per unit subsidy may increase significantly with the circulation of the newspaper. The advantage so conferred would be tantamount to unlimited economies of scale; the higher the circulation the greater per unit subsidy. There would then be an inherent tendency to monopoly, one which could be removed in this instance only by prohibiting newspaper advertising.

very little. And that if they charged extra to cover the costs of any entertainment thrown in with the advertisements, they would hardly sell much more.* They find it far more profitable to provide it free, with or without elements of entertainment, in the hope of recouping from the additional sales and/or higher prices of the products (the results of partial information) the sums they have spent on advertising resources and 'subsidies'. The result is that the newspaper reader is (like the viewer of commercial television) subject to a 'tied sale'. He gets advertising with his news and entertainment whether he wants them together or not; but he gets them both at a price below the cost of the newspaper alone (and, therefore, well below the costs of both newspaper and advertisement).

It may be argued that he prefers this arrangement, since he is not in any case obliged to read the advertisements. Yet the community as a whole is not getting something for nothing. Whatever saving the citizen makes on the purchase of newspapers and advertising together (or on commercial television, viewing and advertising together), comes from the excess of price over the production costs of the advertised products. He does not have the opportunity of paying the full costs, and no more than the full costs, of each of these three things separately – newspapers, advertising, and the advertised products. And, as yet, no economic justification for this anomaly has yet been offered.

An apparent exception to this general argument arises when the manufacturer avails himself of the package or container as a medium for the circulation of his advertisements. Since the costs of circulating such advertisements are virtually nil, this form of 'joint production' of product and advertisement may well appear an efficient means of sales promotion within limits. Nonetheless, since this form of 'joint production' is not unavoidable, consumers' choice can be extended – and the claims of admen tested – by also providing the item without advertisement (save perhaps for the

* Similar remarks apply to cinemas which could charge customers who wished only to see advertisements on the screen, and to television stations which could charge viewers for piping advertisements on to their television screens.

trade name or mark, for identification purposes). Ideally, moreover, both sorts of package or container – those with and those without the advertisement – should be required by law to provide some minimum information. In the case of foodstuffs, for instance, the full list of ingredients would be required. Clearly, the item that carries the advertiser's message would cost more than the same item without the message. They are to be priced accordingly leaving the consumer to choose which he prefers.

The third objection, (c), is similar, on the surface, to the arguments used in justification of state propaganda under a single-party dictatorship. In relation to some issues, the public's preference for partial information may be a fact. One thinks in this connection of religion, of the national myths, beliefs in the inherent goodness of people or in their natural wisdom. Whether it is equally true for the more mundane aspects of life that involve a choice between one model of radiogram and another, one brand of nylon stockings and another, one tin of peaches and another, is more doubtful.*

But one need not be certain that people prefer impartial information before taking action. There can surely be no objection to having partial information of advertisers retailed at a price that covers its cost *along with* impartial information available on exactly the same terms. This is important. As indicated, manufacturers can afford to provide advertising 'free' to the public only because they believe that, by the skilful presentation of partial information, they can so induce a preference for their products as to enable them to recoup their advertising costs by adding them to their production costs, and pricing their goods accordingly. The public then is paying the costs of the advertising without always being aware of paying such costs, and certainly without having any choice in the matter.† If the law were

*When Kallet and Schlink wrote *100,000,000 Guinea Pigs* in 1933 (the number referring to the U.S. population at that time) it was a best-seller for two years. It deeply disturbed the public. President Roosevelt read the book and asked Rex Tugwell, a member of the original brains trust, to draw up a new food and drugs bill.

† True, the public can always save paying such advertising costs by turning to non-advertised, or less advertised, goods. But if it is true that

amended to require manufacturers to sell their advertisements to the public at their full cost, then the public would be enabled to exercise a choice as between buying partial information or impartial information, each at a price covering its full cost to the economy. Only an experiment along these lines could determine whether, indeed, the public preferred partial to impartial information. If the public did opt for a large proportion of partial information about the commercial products they use and a small proportion of impartial information – an unlikely outcome to say the least – the market would see to it that they got what they wanted.

In the meantime it is hard to appreciate the existing law in this country which permits the manufacturer to give out partial and misleading information but does not require him to give specifications of materials used. For such information could be provided by the manufacturer himself far cheaper than it could be unearthed by any impartial research organization. In particular, the absence to this day of a law requiring manufacturers of processed foods to list on the package *all* the ingredients used is regarded by some liberals as little short of scandalous.

(*d*) We turn finally to the fourth possible objection to the abolition of the present system of paid advertisements; the view that the doctrine of freedom of expression should be extended to cover the opinions of advertisers. A difference in the order of social significance between opinions on social, political, and philosophical questions on the one hand, and between opinions concerning the durability of carpets and the qualities of breakfast

---

'it pays to advertise' – and manufacturers certainly act as if they believe it is true, even if it is only to retain their share of the market in the face of other manufacturers' advertising – the non-advertised product will remain relatively unknown. If such a product was as good a quality as the advertised product then it could be sold in the same volume at a lower price. But in an economy which depends on advertising for its information, the public will be unable to avail itself of the advantages of buying unadvertised goods. The more widespread is the information produced by an impartial consumer organization, however, the more will these otherwise little known 'bargains' come to the attention of the public, and the greater will be the saving made by the public.

foods on the other, is sometimes conceded, albeit with the caution that the difference is one of degree and not of kind. There are differences also in the degree of conviction with which the two sets of opinions are held. But there is no need to have the case against freedom to advertise goods turn on these issues.

Milton's eloquent plea for freedom of speech turned on utilitarian considerations: that from the welter of conflicting argument truth would surely emerge. So, perhaps, we should hope that the best kind of filter-tip cigarette and rubber soles will emerge from the competing claims of advertisers! To put it mildly, this does not seem a promising procedure for arriving at the truth in the case of rival commercial products.

For all that, the utilitarian approach is justified. Once we accept the promotion of the public good, in some sense, as the ultimate criterion, we must look on freedom to buy advertising space in the same way as we look on freedom to finance a new business enterprise; as a possible *means* towards realizing the social good. In what way then can the present system of advertising be said to serve the social good? The information it furnishes is, necessarily – indeed, intentionally – partial and incomplete. With the same resources currently used in advertising, impartial and far more extensive information could be provided. (And any alleged public preference for partial information can be tested, as we have already indicated, only by making it available on the market on the same terms as impartial information – which plan itself entails the prohibition of the *existing* system of advertising.)

But even on these economic terms it is hard to give political justification for commercial advertising. Freedom of political expression should be valued primarily not for the truths it discloses, but for the possibility it provides of social change without too much violence. Political doctrines and ideas about social organization evolve over time and in the light of experience. At any moment of time no doctrine or opinion can be held as being absolutely true, or superior to other doctrines or opinions and, if it were believed to be so, it is unlikely that it would remain unchallenged for long. This being the case it is a matter of political expedience to allow men to express their convictions on issues they

125

believe important, persuading others if they can rather than coercing them.

But these considerations do not apply to the claims of advertisers. Advertisers are interested primarily in profits, not in social questions. And the questions they raise – whether one detergent washes whiter than another, whether one make of carpet wears better or has more and thicker pile per square inch than another make, whether one electric blanket provides more warmth, uses less current, or is electrically safer than another type of electric blanket – are not such as to invoke issues of conscience. They do not involve principles for which men are ready to lay down their lives.

What is more, and as distinct from most social questions or questions of conscience, all such questions relevant to consumers' choices can, indeed, be answered impartially and with a high degree of objectivity by a consumer research organization. At the very least it will provide more impartial and more complete information than can be thrown up from the process of competing advertisements. In contrast then to the conflicting claims of ideology, or the conflicting opinions on social policy, there is very little about the competing claims of advertisers that cannot, in all relevant respects, be put to the test. Such claims, that is, can be resolved simply by recourse to the facts.

Part 3 Fallacies About International Trade

10 On American Domination and All That

'Unless our science-based industries are encouraged to find export markets (in Europe) we shall be dominated by the American economy.'

I

Such sweeping allegations can be given clear meaning and analysed in a context uncluttered by habitual controversies only if we start from first principles. Let us illustrate these principles beginning with the uncontroverted fact that the labour force in the United States earns higher real wages than the labour force of any other country – the explanation being simply that, on the average, it is more productive than that of any other country. On the other hand, several countries in Asia whose manufactures are invading our domestic markets and competing with our exports in world markets are among those paying the lowest wages. It would indeed be an unfortunate pattern of circumstances which determined that Britain's trade should be undermined, simultaneously, by the world's highest paid and the world's lowest paid labour; or to put it otherwise, by the technically most productive country and the technically least productive countries. Such a belief might tempt us to adopt a doctrine that Britain should trade only with countries paying their workers 'real' wages exactly equal to those enjoyed by British labour. Such a doctrine, if universally adopted, would solve all the problems of international trade by reducing it to negligible proportions.

Now it happens to be the case that, irrespective of the wages of foreign labour, it is just not possible for a country to be permanently undersold in all traded goods. Moreover, there are simple forces tending over time to balance the overall international trade of any country – the total value of its exports tending to equality with the total value of its imports – at least in the absence of government intervention. These economic propositions are familiar enough to students of the subject, but it may be as well to pause here to persuade the general reader of their validity before returning to the theme of American domination.

It will ease the task of exposition enormously if the reader consents once more to be parted for a while from the complexity of the real world in order to appreciate the simplicity of an imaginary one in which there are but two trading countries, America and Britain. In each of these countries two traded goods only are produced, 'grain' and 'manufactures'. Things will work more smoothly if we suppose that, in so far as international trade is concerned, the governments of both countries are passive; they do not interfere in any way with the trading agreements reached by their merchants. The tale begins with an agreement to exchange $15 for £1 on the exchange market. At this rate of exchange it happens that Britain imports an annual $30 billion-worth of goods, both grain and manufactures, from America. But America imports nothing from Britain in return. One might reasonably regard this hypothetical example as one of complete American domination. But in our smoothly working model it cannot continue for long. For in order to pay for American goods British importers have to buy dollars at the rate of $30 billion per annum. And they will, of course, offer pounds to buy these dollars. American importers, however, are not buying any British goods at the existing dollar-price of pounds. Consequently Americans will not require any pounds to pay for British goods. Obviously the Americans cannot be offering dollars on the foreign exchange market in order to buy pounds. In this foreign exchange market (where dollars are exchanged for pounds and pounds for dollars) there must therefore emerge an *excess* demand for dollars running at the rate of $30 billion per annum (equal at the existing rate of exchange to an *excess supply* of £2 billion). Whether we look at this as a dollar shortage which causes a rise in the (pound) price of the dollar, or as an abundance of pounds which causes a fall in the (dollar) price of the pound, it comes to the same thing: the rate of exchange moves against the pound. It is, however, more conventional to quote a dollar-price of the pound, a convention we adopt here.

Instead of a willingness to give up $15 for £1, Americans will now be ready to pay and the British ready to receive no more than, say, $10 per £1.

What happens when this rate of exchange is established? Since £1-worth of British goods now costs only $10, we can suppose that American importers start to spend $5 billion on British manufactures. And since $15 of American goods now cost £1.5 (as compared with only £1 at the old exchange rate) British importers reduce their demand for American goods, and therefore their demand for dollars to, say, $20 billion.

Why do we imagine that the Americans, with their lower wage costs in every internationally traded good, will buy anything at all from Britain when British goods become cheaper in terms of dollars? The reason is simple: even though Americans can produce everything at a lower wage cost than Britain their cost advantage is unlikely to be equally great in the production of each and every good. In our example, America's cost advantage in grain is taken to be much greater than her cost advantage in manufactures. Therefore, once the pound becomes cheap enough in American dollars, Americans will begin to import manufactures from Britain. In general, Americans will begin to import – as the pound becomes cheaper to them – those goods in which their cost advantage is least. In exchange, Americans will be exporting those goods in which their cost advantage is greatest. We suppose, therefore, that at this new rate of exchange British imports still exceed her exports by $15 billion (or by £1.5 billion). There remains an excess demand for dollars of $15 billion and, sooner or later, another revision of the exchange rate will take place in favour of the dollar as against the pound. Clearly these movements in the rate of exchange, in response to an excess of imports over exports for either country (the reverse being true of the other country), comprise the price-mechanism which operates to bring the over-all balance of trade into equilibrium. Indeed, a smoothly operating foreign exchange market would be a prime example of a sensitive feedback mechanism: the larger the foreign trade disequilibrium arising from any autonomous change in taste or technology – the larger, say, the excess demand for dollars – the more powerful the force tending to return to equilibrium.

We could bring into the picture any number of countries, and therefore any number of currencies, without any essential modification of this mechanism, and without any modification of the significant result that there will be a continuously operating tendency to establish a set of exchange rates between the various currencies at which the value of total imports and exports of each country is in balance.

II

Still maintaining the fiction that there is a highly organized foreign exchange market in which the values of all currencies are being continually revised – a system of 'flexible exchanges' in the parlance of economists – let us take a first plausible step towards the thesis of American economic domination by imagining that America takes a big technical stride forward, one that enables her to reduce the price (or improve the quality) of her midget computers. America now begins to sell more midget computers to Britain – and the alarm bells sound all over Europe. But what of it? If, at the *provisionally unchanged* rate of exchange, Britain *spends* more on American computers than before, her resulting excess demand for dollars will turn the rate of exchange against Britain, making the dollar dearer in terms of the pound, so acting to restore the balance of payments. Whether Britain will, on balance, be better or worse off than before can be decided only by weighing the advantage of buying a larger number of American computers at a lower pound-price than before against the disadvantage of paying somewhat more (in pounds) for all the other goods imported from America in consequence of the induced rise in the price of the dollar. But there is another possibility. Britain, at the old rate of exchange, may *spend* less than before on American computers even though she purchases a greater number than before. If, say, the dollar-price of American computers falls by twenty per cent and Britain buys only ten per cent more computers than before, the total dollar bill for computers will be smaller than before. Britain's total demand for dollars will therefore fall and the rate of exchange will move in her favour: which is to say the dollar will cost less in terms of pounds and all other American goods will be cheaper in pounds than before. In this case, that of an 'inelastic' demand for American computers, there is a clear advantage to Britain in America's technological advance.

Let us now introduce a little more realism. If Britain also were producing midget computers for the domestic market, then although all *users* of computers in Britain would stand to gain, firms in Britain would have to contract output or close down. Some workers engaged in the production of computers would initially be out of employment. Thus some labour and capital would have to move out of computer production into some other economic activity. Although this is indeed the solution called for we must face up to the possibility that hardship may be suffered in the process of closing down factories and transferring workers to other employment. Measures designed to increase the mobility of labour such as travel and housing subsidies, and retraining facilities, will go some way to mitigating hardship, as also will higher unemployment pay. Be that as it may, this hardship associated with redirecting our resources to fit in with the changing pattern of demand and technology has no particular connection with American technological advance. In a country which engaged in no foreign trade at all, the overall changing pattern of demand and technology would also require expansion of some industries and contraction of others, though possibly to a lesser extent than in a country competing in world markets.

III

Now consider a more relevant complication. An American advantage in computer production may arise not from some technical innovation, but from the great size of the American computer industry, a size which can be maintained only by a market as large and wealthy as the American market. If it happened to be true that the larger the scale of production the lower

133

the cost of computer production, then a country like America, that is already producing far more computers than any other country, has a cost advantage to start with. In the absence of obstacles to international trade, this cost advantage would get larger as American computers successfully penetrated other markets. Indeed, in the limiting case, only one giant computer plant would be needed to supply the world's current computer requirements, and if America happened to have the largest plant to start with, this initial advantage would determine its location there rather than in any of the other economically advanced countries.

Now it is doubtful whether, even in computer or aircraft production, the economies of large-scale production are as large as this. The products for which the British home market, alone, is too small to exploit really significant economies of large-scale production must be very few indeed.* But even if we suppose that the economies of large-scale production are virtually unlimited, what follows? Because of its sheer size, America may have a head start; in which case Britain and other countries import computers from America and contribute thereby to reducing computer costs further. If, in the event, Britain chooses to follow this policy it is possible, again, that the rate of exchange will tend to move either in favour or against the pound (depending on the 'elasticity' of our demand for computers). And even if it does move against the pound, thereby raising the price of our other imports, it is nonetheless possible – as has been argued in the preceding

---

*At this point the reader may be thinking of the *Concorde* supersonic airliner. This is not, strictly speaking, a case of economies of scale, though one related to the size of the enterprise nevertheless. In order to produce any number at all of this complex product requires financial and technical resources of no small order. And though there is no doubt that either Britain or France alone could have produced a supersonic airliner of the *Concorde* size, or larger, it was believed an advantage to pool resources and to share the inevitable market risks. Whether any positive return can be expected from this particular joint investment project seems doubtful at the moment of writing. Questions of prestige aside, if we must have supersonic airliners, it may have been economically wiser to have left their development to the Americans.

134

section – that there will be net economic advantages as compared with a policy of protection against American computer exports. It is, however, always possible for Britain to ensure unambiguous advantage from any reduction in American prices simply by adopting a quota system for computers. In that way, although Britain might respond to any cost reduction by increasing computer purchases from America, she could always ensure that in total she *spent* less than before on them. The rate of exchange would then move in favour of the pound: all American goods would be cheaper in pounds.

IV

The final complication we must consider is that arising if Britain is competing with America in third markets as an exporter of computers. In that case America gains some technological advantage and, possibly, causes the rate of exchange to move against Britain. But it is not likely to be long-lasting. New technological processes do not remain secret for very long and are usually available to other firms in any country on patent. Over time, small technological advantages in the production of scores of goods are likely to swing from one trading country to another. It is not impossible that, in several important lines of production, America will be setting the technical pace for some time and that Britain and other European countries may suffer a reduced share (though not necessarily a reduced *volume* of sales) in third markets as well as in the American market. The same result follows for any internationally traded good enjoying virtually unlimited economies of scale in which America has a head start.*

*However, in so far as America is competing within third markets from which we import, there can be counterbalancing advantages to Britain. If, for example, American technological progress in certain manufactures is such that Britain exports fewer manufactures to Australia, it is also likely that Australia ends up importing a greater value of goods than before. It then has to lower its export prices (or reduce the value of the Australian dollar relative to all other currencies). Britain will then benefit from buying cheaper Australian wool and other things.

This is about the most that can be wrung from the American-domination theme: a reduction of our exports to third markets and, therefore, of our total exports relative to our imports, an event requiring a fall in the pound relative to foreign currencies in order to restore balance in our international trade. To British residents this implies a rise in the pound-prices of imported goods.* But when the worst that is imagined takes place, a rise in import prices over time is not likely to do more than reduce the gradual rise in 'real' *per capita* income over time. And when one considers in the light of American experience how slight is the real benefit of further increases in 'real' income in a country as wealthy as Britain,† the concern over the so-called economic domination of America is hardly warranted.

Even this 'worst imaginable' view has, however, to be modified once we move from tracing the effects of just one of several technical advances in America to tracing the effects of a continual flow of superior technical innovations. A more rapid rate of technological advance in America than in Britain would have one really important consequence on the balance of payments, additional to those already discussed. For it implies that *per capita* 'real' income is growing at a faster rate in America than in Britain. Since imports rise with 'real' income, a faster rise in American 'real' income (compared with British 'real' income) acts to raise American imports over time faster than the rise of British imports. This 'real' income effect of faster technical progress therefore tends to worsen the American balance of payments at the expense of an improvement in the British balance of payments. It therefore acts over time to turn the terms of trade in Britain's favour – that is, it tends to make Britain's imports cheaper.

v

It is quite possible, however, that what many people are chiefly concerned about is the employment of scientists and technicians

* Other than the pound-price of the particular American goods whose costs have fallen owing to technological progress.

† See Chapter 21.

in this country. There is a fear that if America undertakes to sell an increasing proportion of those goods requiring big inputs of scientific talent we shall not have sufficient employment for scientists and technicians: and, of course, we are very superstitious about losing such people. As we have already observed, however, there is a correcting mechanism at work over time which ensures that Britain maintains her exports at the cost, at worst, of her imports rising in price. But even if during such readjustment over time it emerges that America has some comparative advantage in the production of the most highly technological goods – so that, in equilibrium, Britain's exports tend to become less science-using than American exports – the direct effect on the employment requirements in Britain of scientists and technicians may be small compared with their inducement to emigrate to America. Indeed our stock of scientists and engineers over the future is almost certain to be reduced much more by emigration to America than by America's increased specialization in 'science-based' industries.

One might add in passing, however, that the loss suffered by any country from the emigration of its scientists and engineers has been grossly over-stated.* Nevertheless, if we wish to place a value on the services of scientists beyond that imputed to them by the market, there is nothing to stop us from translating our convictions into direct subsidies to scientists in order to maintain their services, or even to increase them, in chosen fields of research, while at the same time continuing to trade freely with the rest of the world.

Taking the quoted passage, which heads the chapter, as my text, I have attacked a particular fallacy connected with the frequent allegation of American economic domination: the fear of our being undersold in world markets unless, somehow, we can keep pace with advancing American technology. There can, of course, be other ideas associated with the term 'American economic domination'; for example, the growth of American business investment in British industry – which is, however,

* See Chapter 17.

accompanied by growing British, and West European, investment in the United States.

If a country is interested primarily in material standards, the more foreign long-term capital it attracts the better. As for vague but persistent fears of control, the decisions taken by foreign businessmen and managers, guided as they are by pecuniary considerations, are no different in kind from those taken by indigenous businessmen and managers.

If the foreign investor wishes to withdraw his capital from Britain, all he can do is sell his shares, or his titles to direct ownership of assets in Britain, to others. Regardless of who owns them, however, the plant, machinery, buildings, and mines in Britain continue to remain in Britain. We need not worry about their being packed up and sent abroad. Indeed, so long as Britain remains a sovereign power, the control of industry as a whole, and of any particular industry or firm in Britain, irrespective of ownership, comes within the jurisdiction of British laws.

VI

A Postscript – The assumption of freely flexible exchange rates, determined in world markets, has been maintained throughout the argument for simplicity of exposition: for in the long run a country which does not erect permanent barriers to trade must be tending to balanced trade through a change in its price level relative to those of other countries. If we begin with a disequilibrium in which Britain has an excess of imports, the relative fall in her price level necessary to restore balance is accomplished most easily by a fall in the value of the pound in terms of other currencies. It is a harder and slower process to achieve the same effect by deflationary measures that are more likely to reduce employment than to reduce wages – or, at best, to restrain them long enough in the hope that wages abroad will rise, so raising foreign prices relative to British prices.* The more inflexible (to

*The observation that unpredictable exchange rates would have to be met by hedging operations on the forward exchange market which would add to the cost, and therefore reduce the volume, of international trade

downward adjustment at least) are money wage rates, the stronger the case for flexible exchange rates. And in a country where real *per capita* income has been rising steadily over time there is the need both for increased flexibility and the necessary margin of wealth that makes it possible. (*a*) The need for increased flexibility arises simply because the proportion of expenditure that is 'luxury' expenditure rises with the increase over time of *per capita* 'real' income, a consequence which results in more impulse- and fashion-buying. The patterns of demand over a growing range of goods become more volatile and less predictable. One may expect that a good deal of international trade becomes increasingly fickle and the consequent need for adjustments more frequent. (*b*) The *practicability* of increased flexibility arises directly from the rise in *per capita* 'real' income: the wealthier people become, the better able they are to sustain small ups and downs in their standard of living without genuine hardship.

Since both the need and the practicability for increased flexibility spring from the same cause, the rise in *per capita* 'real' income over time, ordinary wisdom would have led one to expect government policies making for increased flexibility, in this way minimizing the need for continual government intervention. Yet the contrary tendencies are observed to be at work. Increasing government intervention is leading to increasing rigidities. The attempts to maintain rigid exchange rates are accompanied by a vast number of controls needed to enforce them. A National Incomes Board in Britain adds rigidity to wage-differentials. And the post-war obsession in the country at large with cost-of-living indices makes temporary (downward) accommodation, even in the smallest degree, all but impossible. If the British economy

---

can hardly be rated as a serious objection. One has only to consider the large number of trade-restrictive measures, which all countries resort to, in maintaining the international value of their currencies – at the fixed parities which are alleged by governments to be in the interests of expanding international trade – to appreciate the absurdity of the argument. There are other costs of maintaining fixed parities: consider the costs to the British exchequer of the high interest rates that are paid on foreign-owned sterling balances in the repeated endeavours to discourage the owners from exchanging them for dollars or other currencies. (See Chapter 12.)

appears repeatedly to be running into trouble, it is not because of any inherent weakness in the structure. Nor is it because the economy is not growing fast enough.* It is simply because it is developing arthritic institutions: there is not enough flexibility in the economic machinery.

*See Chapter 19.

11 On the Pound being in Danger

'When the pound is in danger the country is in danger.'

I

'The pound is in danger' has something in it of a rallying cry – or rather it might have if governments were not so prone to be harking back to the spirit of Dunkirk at every other mini-crisis.

Let us first be clear on the nature of the danger. It is far from mortal. It is nothing more than 'pressure' in the foreign exchange markets tending to reduce the price of the pound in terms of foreign currencies. If the pound does fall it will, initially at least, fall in terms of *all* other currencies. A pound will then buy fewer marks, dollars, francs, pesetas, escudos, rupees, etc., than before. Consequently all our imported goods will become dearer. But it will simplify matters in this chapter if we choose a single currency, the dollar, to represent all other currencies.

In an 'equilibrium' situation, the current *demand for dollars* (by sterling holders who seek to exchange their holdings of pounds for dollars) is equal – at the existing exchange rate, say, £1 equal to $2.40 – to the demand for pounds by dollar-holders. But, as this latter demand for pounds by dollar-holders can just as well be described as an offer by these dollar-holders to *supply dollars* in exchange for pounds, we can conveniently talk of the supply of dollars (by dollar-holders) being equal, in equilibrium, to the current demand for dollars (by sterling-holders). At any rate, we shall stick to this way of describing the operation of the foreign exchange market – that is, the demand for and the supply of dollars – in order to avoid possible confusion.

The pressure on the pound we are talking of can then be seen to arise from the demand (by holders of pounds sterling) for more dollars than the actual amounts of dollars being offered by dollar-holders at the existing rate of exchange. Put briefly, the demand for dollars exceeds the supply of dollars at the going rate of exchange. Put more briefly yet, there is an *excess* demand for dollars.

Now it is a familiar economic proposition that an excess demand for anything *tends* to raise its price. An excess demand for dollars therefore *tends* to raise the price of the dollar in terms of pounds – or, put the other way round, to lower the price of a pound in terms of dollars, e.g. from $2.40 for a pound to $2.00 for a pound. The fear of such a fall in the dollar-price of a pound – or, more briefly, a fall in the pound – is this thing the government is warning us about. If it takes place, a dollar's worth of goods will cost us more – in shillings – than before.

We emphasized the word *tends* in the preceding paragraph, because the downward pressure exerted on the pound may be resisted. In fact the trouble starts just because the British government endeavours to resist the mounting pressure on the pound – that is, the continuing excess demand for dollars – by entering the market and supplying the excess demand for dollars from its own vast holdings of dollar balances. But the government's holdings of dollars – roughly £1,000 millions'-worth – though large compared with daily or weekly transactions in the foreign exchange market, are not unlimited. Unless the government can borrow dollars from foreign banks, or the excess demand for dollars by holders of sterling comes to an end in time, the government's holdings will become depleted. The excess demand for dollars can then no longer be offset by the additional supply of dollars put on the market by the government, and the dollar-price of the pound will indeed start to fall.

If this happens our dollar imports will become dearer – they will cost more in pounds than before. On the other hand, *provided* that the prices of the goods we export do not change, they will cost less in dollars than before. But if our imports from America cost us more (in pounds) than before, we should import a smaller volume of American goods. And if our exports cost the Americans less (in dollars) than before they will generally buy more, and therefore the volume of our exports should rise.*

* It is, of course, possible to raise the (pound) prices of our exports a little thereby increasing our sales abroad *less* than if we had, instead,

142

Finally, provided the response to the domestic price of imports in both countries is large enough, this fall in the dollar-price of the pound will act to restore equilibrium. In that case, American importers will be *offering more dollars* to pay for their larger purchases of cheaper (in dollars) British goods, and/or British importers will be *demanding fewer dollars* to pay for their smaller purchases of dearer (in pounds) American goods. Without further government intervention, then, the excess demand for dollars will disappear once the dollar-price of the pound falls sufficiently. And the greater the response in both countries to a fall in the dollar-price of the pound, the smaller this fall needs to be to restore equilibrium.

II

We must now ask ourselves how the excess demand for dollars arises in the first place. It can arise in two different ways:

(*a*) More than other governments, the British government is in debt to other countries. The very rough figure to bear in mind is £4 billion – of which about two thirds is held by foreign governments, the remainder being held by private firms and individuals. One can easily picture foreigners, both individuals and governments, having large sterling balances in British banks which add up to the above figure. It is more realistic, however, to suppose that, at any moment of time, foreigners hold only a fraction of this amount on current account in British banks, the larger part being invested in British securities – mainly interest-bearing short-term securities and bills issued by the British government. In this form they earn an income for their holders, while being easily convertible if necessary into cash.

In ordinary times, foreign holders of sterling balances (in which term we shall include from now on holdings also of

---

maintained their prices unchanged. If foreign purchases of certain goods are not likely to increase very much following a fall in the pound, their sale will fetch fewer dollars than before. In such cases – where foreign demand is insensitive to the price – one can maintain dollar earnings from such goods by raising the pound-price accordingly.

British short-term securities) are quite content to go on holding these balances. In times of 'crisis', however, they may begin to worry about the dollar value of their sterling balances, or discern the possibility of capital gains while incurring little risk. Crisis, here, means devaluation – a fall in the dollar-price of the pound. They will look at things this way: suppose the pound does fall, from its existing rate $2.40 to $2.00, and they hold on to their pounds. They will then be able to get only $2,000 for every £1,000 whenever they need dollars (to buy American goods or services), instead of the $2,400 they could have got before devaluation. If, then, there is any likelihood of devaluation, they would be advised to exchange their pounds for dollars before it takes place – that is, at the existing rate of $2.40 for each pound.

Moreover, even if they have little or no use at all for dollars there is an incentive to exchange their pounds for dollars at the existing rate of $2.40. For if the devaluation does take place, they can make a capital gain: exchanging their sterling into dollars, every £1,000 before devaluation will fetch $2,400. Once the devaluation takes place and the dollar-price of the pound is $2.00, they can exchange their dollars for sterling. For every $2,400 they will get, not just £1,000 as before, but £1,200. This is a capital gain of £200 on every £1,000 or a profit of twenty per cent, usually over a short period, and is a very respectable return for so slight an effort. Obviously it is a highly attractive option since there is practically no risk run. If they are wrong and devaluation does not take place nothing is lost but the relatively small charges incurred in transferring funds from one currency into another. In fact they would only be running a risk if there was a good chance that the price of the pound would *rise* as well as fall.

But in this sort of crisis such a risk does not arise. Everyone knows that the government is running down its reserves of dollars in an attempt to prevent the pound falling. If the government succeeds, the pound does not fall. But it certainly does not rise; so one cannot lose. However, it may fall and, indeed, simply by demanding more dollars – so further depleting the government's dollar reserves – one makes some small contribution to bringing about the desired fall, and so assures oneself of a gain.

The reader may now appreciate why such 'speculation' on the foreign exchange is regarded as parasitic; and also why it is so attractive, there being only a one-way option – 'you can't lose.' He will also appreciate why the rumour of an impending devaluation may go far to bring it about. Both groups, those who fear for the dollar value of their money as well as those who seek capital gains, will rush to convert pounds into dollars. It is not even necessary to hold sterling balances in the first place. Speculative gains can be made by *borrowing* sterling, generally from British banks. For every £1,000 an American can borrow, he can convert at once into $2,400, wait for devaluation of the pound to $2, and then spend only $2,000 of it in repaying the British bank its £1,000. This leaves him a profit of $400 (less any interest charges). Unless, then, there are effective checks on British banks lending for such purposes, the demand for dollars by speculators whenever the pound is 'in danger' can reach irresistible proportions. In the meantime the British government, who for one reason or another wants to hold the rate of exchange at $2.40 to the pound, has to dig ever deeper into its dollar holdings and possibly, also, to borrow large sums of dollars from American banks (in general, from many West European Central Banks also) in order to continue its operation of supplying the growing excess demand for dollars and preventing it from depressing the pound.

(b) The excess demand for dollars, on the other hand, can arise wholly from current trade. If, at the going rate of exchange, Britain tends to import a greater value of goods and services than she exports, then the demand for dollars by British importers (who have to pay American merchants in dollars) exceeds the supply of dollars earned by British exporters. In the absence of the government using its vast holdings of dollars to meet the current excess demand for dollars, the dollar price of the pound would, again, start to decline.

There can also be an excess current demand for dollars in exchange for pounds from the other countries of the Sterling Area –

i.e., those countries that have elected to use their sterling balances as central bank reserves and as a means of payment for their international debts. When the *rest* of the Sterling Area (the Sterling Area without Britain) as a whole exports to non-Sterling Area countries, the dollars it earns are generally added to Britain's dollar reserves. When the rest of the Sterling Area imports from non-Sterling Area countries, it uses up Britain's dollar reserves. If this area's imports and exports are currently in balance it makes no difference to Britain's dollar reserves. But if its imports exceed its exports, the sterling balances of the rest of the Sterling Area as a whole are run down in buying the dollars necessary to meet its import surplus. The use of some of its sterling to buy these dollars constitutes an excess demand for dollars on the foreign exchange market. And, in order to prevent a decline in the dollar-price of the pound, the Bank of England will have to meet this excess demand for dollars from its reserves of dollar holdings.

The significance of all this is simply that balanced trade by Britain alone does not ensure that there will be no excess current demand for dollars arising in the course of international trade. Britain might well be in current balance-of-payments equilibrium, it may even be enjoying an export surplus, yet – because of an excess of imports from the non-Sterling Area by the rest of the Sterling Area – there can still be, on balance, an excess demand for dollars; one which could conceivably continue year after year until the sterling balances of these countries were entirely used up. In attempting to maintain the dollar-price of the pound under these circumstances, Britain would have to use up more and more of her dollar reserves.

Though this is a possibility to bear in mind, it so happens that in recent years, the rest of the Sterling Area as a whole has been adding to Britain's dollar reserves rather than drawing on them. In other words, these countries have been selling more to the non-Sterling Area than they have been buying from it. The greater part of their excess dollar earnings have been handed over to Britain in exchange for pounds, and some part of these accumulating pounds are then transferred to British traders in payment of their excess imports from Britain.

146

On the Pound being in Danger

III

It need hardly be pointed out that both the capital, or 'speculative', transactions and the current trade transactions can operate, and are in fact likely to operate, simultaneously. News about a persistent 'adverse' balance of trade – the value of current imports exceeding that of exports – and the consequent reduction in the government's holdings of dollars necessary to prevent a fall in the pound may start fears, and hopes, of an eventual fall in the dollar-price of the pound. Foreign holders of sterling, and indeed all businessmen with balances either in British banks or able to borrow from British banks who can also get permission to convert into dollars, will be anxious to convert into dollars, thereby vastly increasing the difficulties of maintaining the dollar-price of the pound.

Again, however, we should be clear about the magnitudes involved. Annual British trade deficits of two or three hundred million pounds – the excess of our imports over our exports – may seem large in absolute terms, or in comparison with our reserves of dollars (or of gold and other foreign currencies). But it is misleading to talk about a crisis unless the deficit is large in relation to our total resources. In fact trade deficits seldom approach two per cent of our total national output. Over the last few years it has averaged between £250 million and £400 million, or about one per cent of our national output. The notion, therefore, that we are – or ever were – struggling for 'national survival' is patent nonsense; and such expressions are passing strange in a country generally given to understatement. The extra goods we should have to export to come into balance could, indeed, be supplied two to three times over merely from the average annual increase of our national output: an average three per cent growth rate adds, each year, about £900 millions of additional goods to our total national output. We could give away a quarter, or if necessary, a half of this extra without enduring the least hardship.

Of course, we can admit to difficulties in coaxing foreigners to buy those two or three hundred millions' worth extra of our goods in addition to the £6,000 millions' worth they already buy. But if

147

they are willing to buy the extra, we should be put to little inconvenience in supplying them. Indeed, we should be put to little inconvenience in reaching trade balance in another way; cutting down our imports by two to three hundred million pounds – whether of 'luxuries', foreign securities or government purchases abroad. But whether we attempt one method or another to restore trade balance – and the fashion these days is to choose that which hurts the most; deflating the economy in the hope of expanding exports – neither the magnitude of the deficit compared with our resources, nor the consequences of failing to achieve it by present methods, have anything like the repercussions on the material well-being of the country that could warrant the creation of a sense of crisis.

12 On Hard Work Strengthening the Pound

'Harder work is the only cure for the weakness of sterling.'

The reader who has assimilated the contents of the preceding chapter will have some idea of the interpretation to put on the dramatic announcement that 'sterling is in danger' or 'under heavy pressure'. He will, I hope, be convinced at least that our survival as a nation, or even as a viable economy, is in no way menaced, and that the problem arises from trying to maintain the dollar-price of the pound at a time when the demand for pounds is falling off (or, put otherwise, there is an excess demand for dollars).

So what is to be done? Working harder may be good for the soul, perhaps also for the constitution. It may well result in a greater national output which, as all growthmen will affirm, is an excellent thing in itself. But does it quite meet the situation? After all, what people work harder than the Americans? Their productivity is the highest in the world, as also is the incidence of ulcers among their executives. And yet, at the time of writing (April 1968), they have run into very bad balance-of-payments weather. Greed and sweat – or, more politely, ambition and effort – are apparently not enough.

But to an economist, a simple answer is no answer. So let us consider the possible remedies to a sterling crisis brought on by (*a*) a speculative flight from sterling, and by (*b*) a deficit in the current balance of trade.

(*a*) If there is very little wrong with the current trade balance except that, for one reason or another, holders of sterling, and particularly foreign holders of sterling, are prone to 'lose con-

149

fidence in sterling' (i.e. they expect the dollar-price of sterling to decline) too often, what counter-measures are open to us?

(*i*) There is, first, the standard response of British governments since the war: paying higher interest rates so as to tempt foreign holders of short-term securities to hold on to them. This response can be expensive for the British tax-payer who has to meet the amounts necessary to pay the additional interest charges. It has, moreover, two clear disadvantages.

One is that foreign holders of convertible sterling balances may be 'bribed' for the nonce to continue holding their money in sterling securities if their fears, or hopes, of a fall in the dollar-price of sterling are not too strong. But such 'crises of confidence' are easily enough caused: a firm denial of a rumour by a minor minister is usually enough and, so long as convertible sterling balances amounting to £4,000 million continue to be held by foreigners, such balances will – regardless of the rate of interest – continue to remain a threat to the official maintenance of the price of the pound.*

---

*Businessmen engaged in foreign trade may also be instrumental – through what is known as 'leads and lags' – in bringing pressure to bear on the dollar-price of the pound. A British exporter to the United States will normally sell the dollars he earns as soon as he receives them. If, however, he expects the dollar-price of the pound to fall very soon, he will delay selling his dollar proceeds to British banks in the hope that devaluation will take place. If it does, if the price of the pound falls from $2.40 to $2.00, then for every $240 he has to his credit in the United States he will receive £120. Compared with the £100 he would have received at the old rate ($2.40), he now makes £20 more, or twenty per cent profit. In anticipation of such a gain, he 'lags' the supply of his dollars to the Bank of England, and this temporary reduction of the dollar supply tends to weaken the dollar-price of the pound.

Under the same circumstances, the British importer has an incentive to pay pounds for dollar goods as early as possible – perhaps well in advance of receiving such goods from America – for fear of having to pay £120 for each $240 worth of American goods if the pound falls to $2.00 (compared with the £100 he pays for $240 worth of American goods at the existing rate of exchange). In anticipation of an early devaluation, therefore, the British importer tends to advance, or 'lead' his demand for dollars, again weakening the pound.

In addition to leads and lags, there are clandestine capital movements

The other, and potentially greater, disadvantage of this popular counter-measure is that it can act to reduce the level of total employment in the domestic economy. High interest rates tend to reduce aggregate domestic expenditure – both consumption expenditure and investment expenditure. It may well be the case, as it has been since the war, that aggregate domestic expenditure has a tendency to outrun aggregate capacity and is therefore inflationary. In that case, these higher interest rates tend also to reduce aggregate domestic expenditure and so reduce inflationary pressure. But it is just as possible for a speculative crisis to take place when the British economy is depressed – when in fact aggregate domestic demand is well below the available productive capacity of the economy, and there is therefore widespread unemployment. In that case, the standard recourse to high interest rates and 'tight money' would reduce business investment and act to aggravate the depression.

(*ii*) An alternative counter-measure consists of arrangements to 'freeze' all, or the more volatile part, of these, convertible sterling balances, by the simple expedient of making them – overnight, and without warning – 'non-transferable'. The holders of such sterling balances could not then pay sterling to other persons without official consent. Less drastic, such sterling balances could be made inconvertible into other currencies – the owners would not be permitted to exchange them on the market for dollars. This measure would certainly eliminate the downward pressure on the pound in the official foreign exchange market – though it might result in the operation of a 'black market', one in which people exchange pound cheques for dollar cheques

---

which weaken the pound. By understating the value of exports to the United States by, say, $1,000, the British exporter makes a private arrangement with the American importer to place this extra $1,000 in an American account. The Bank of England receives dollars equivalent only to the understated value on the invoice. The British importer is also in a position to 'export capital' simply by over-stating the value of the American goods he imports, having an agreement with the American exporter to put the difference to the British importer's secret American account. Thus a demand for dollars in excess of the true value of the imports into Britain also acts to weaken the pound.

privately, and at a dollar-price for sterling below the official rate. If the volatile part of the foreign-held sterling balances were made inconvertible into dollars the government could at some later date either enter into an agreement with official foreign holders of sterling to release each year a certain amount of their sterling balances for conversion into dollars, or other foreign currencies, or else allow these balances to be used, up to some limiting amount each year, to buy British goods until, over a period, they were entirely used up. A more likely outcome of such negotiations would be a combination of both.*

(*iii*) Over a long period Britain could attempt gradually to 'neutralize' the foreign-held sterling balances simply by accumulating short-term balances of dollars or other currencies to an equal value. Thus, if over a period we had a favourable balance of payments – exports of goods and services exceeding imports – the government could, instead of raising the dollar-price of sterling, allow this annual excess supply of dollars earned either to accumulate in American banks partly on current account, partly on deposit account, or use the annual excess dollar earnings to buy short-term securities. Having suceeded in building up our dollar reserves to a value about equal to our sterling liabilities, we should be able to meet any sudden demands for dollars by foreign sterling-holders without having to borrow from foreign Central Banks.

It should be made clear, however, that unless the British government made arrangements to transfer to itself the dollars earned by exporters, they might easily be transferred to other British subjects who would use them to buy long-term dollar securities over which the British government would have no immediate control. In fact there already exist enough British-held foreign securities which, if they were to be sold on the instant in

---

*Some writers profess a moral opposition to the idea of a unilateral freezing of the sterling balances prior to reaching long-term arrangements for redeeming them. Though I am concerned here only with what is technically practicable, one cannot feel very happy over the course of events resulting from the inflexible Treasury policy – officials proclaiming that sterling would not be devalued right up to the day planned for its devaluation.

foreign markets, would yield more than enough to meet the demands for dollars (or for other foreign currencies) by foreign holders of sterling in any emergency. The government could, if it wished, appropriate these British-held foreign securities in an emergency (in return for inconvertible sterling balances to their owners), but is reluctant to do so for political and economic reasons. These long-term foreign securities earn more over time for the British holders than does the value of all the short-term British securities held by foreigners; and this arrangement makes some annual contribution to the current balance of payments.

These alternative measures by which we could meet a speculative run on sterling do not, of course, preclude our working harder. But even if harder work were in any degree efficacious the results would not be likely to make themselves felt in the few days or weeks over which we ride out the crisis. We shall, however, discuss this Samuel Smiles prescription for overcoming our economic troubles in the next section, where it is more appropriately treated in connection with a sterling crisis arising from a persistent balance-of-payments deficit.

II

(b) We now consider the second cause of 'pressure on the pound': that arising from the current excess of our imports over our exports. In the absence of any pressure exerted by foreign holders of sterling balances, the excess of our imports over our exports would entail an excess demand for dollars which, as already indicated, tends to raise the pound-price of dollars; or, to put it the other way round, tends to lower the dollar-price of the pound. Let us briefly consider the alternative methods for dealing with a persistent import surplus.

(i) Without fears of retaliation from other countries we could cut down our expenditure on two categories of foreign goods and services. Our military expenditure abroad is one of these. How much we spend abroad is, of course, determined through the political process. But so, ultimately, is the decision on how to restore the balance of payments. Since Britain continues to bear a

153

far greater overseas military expenditure than any other West European country, there is at least a case for investigating the political consequences of making further economies.

The other category is the expenditure on foreign assets, which include purchases of long-term securities or direct purchases of a share in new foreign investments.* Such purchases of foreign assets, which may appear desirable in the longer term, since the interest or dividends earned on them add to our earnings of dollars, are in no sense necessary in the short run. It may well be that in the absence of these 'imports' of foreign assets the trade deficit would vanish or be substantially reduced. The gross amount spent abroad by British investors varies greatly from year to year. An average figure of between £300 million and £400 million over the last six years provides a rough idea of the value of these foreign purchases which could be controlled, or completely prohibited for a time, without inflicting any hardship on the citizen.†

Apart from these non-retaliatory items there is a vast range of imported goods which by no stretch of the imagination could be called essential. Calls for sacrifices for the 'exports that are necessary for our survival' must sound absurd once we start looking at the kind of imports we are supposed to be struggling to pay for by our exports. They include luxury goods, fashion goods, and goods that are close substitutes for British goods and materials: such things are German and Italian cars, Belgian and Dutch chocolate, Japanese cameras and toys, Italian shoes, French lingerie, wines and cheeses, Dutch butter and tomatoes, and a wide variety of chemicals and machinery that compete

*A large part of our annual investment in foreign assets arises from profits made on existing foreign investments which, instead of being sold for sterling, are re-invested abroad.

†In addition to this figure for private investment abroad, the British government spends at the annual rate of some £200 million in aid to poor countries, about half of which is on capital account. A conservative estimate of the 'untied' proportion of this aid would be about one third. Not only therefore do we have to supply £130–40 million direct to such countries, we have also to sell between £60 million and £70 million to 'hard' currency countries.

closely with those produced in this country. They may well be desirable, but they are certainly not necessary to our survival. Certain groups of people might feel resentful if deprived of them, but their suspension would not cause hardship. We could call them expendable, bearing in mind that the dividing line is very blurred indeed. At a very rough guess their magnitude would be in the region of a billion pounds per annum.

If quotas were imposed on such items so as to limit the quantity imported in any year, the supplying countries might well take offence. But if it were made clear that the quotas were temporary only, and were the only means (short of devaluation or deflation) of ensuring that we did not buy more abroad than we sold, there would be no reasonable case for retaliation – which is not to say there would not be any. Retaliation would be less likely, however, if the quotas were directed towards those countries with which our trade deficit was largest.

III

(*ii*) We come at last to the homely exhortation that we should work harder. And perhaps we should do so for a number of reasons. What is at issue, however, is whether this is an efficient method of restoring equilibrium in our balance of payments.

The existing conditions of work depend upon the stock of capital goods in the country, upon technology, management, climate and custom, along with government intervention and trade-union bargaining. Considerations of the balance of payments do not seem to have entered into their determination. However, let us suppose that everyone decides to 'back Britain' and work harder. What results is it reasonable to anticipate?

About two-fifths of the working population are to be found in what are called 'tertiary' or service industries. They work in hotels or restaurants or in domestic service, or are employed in commerce, education, the civil service, show business or the retail trade. It is not clear how all of such people could work harder, or what difference it would make to our trade balance if they did. If hoteliers tried harder they might attract more tourists. On the other hand if retailers opened later hours they might sell more imports.

Of the remainder of the working population employed in industry, agriculture, mining and transport, those employed on *piece rates* would, if they worked harder, collect more pay. Those employed on *time rates*, on the other hand, would be able to work harder without receiving additional remuneration. Though this seems inequitable, it is to the efforts of this latter group we must turn for any discernible effect on the trade balance.

Supplying effectively more labour for the same wage reduces the wage cost per unit of output produced. Initially this entails greater profit. The firm has the choice therefore of any of a combination of the following: increasing its dividend reserves which will raise its share prices and provide capital gains for shareholders; actually paying out higher dividends to shareholders; increasing its investment in new plant and machinery, which also improves the future dividend prospects of shareholders; raising wages, or lowering prices. The government may prevent higher dividends or wages, but it is still not certain that prices will be lowered. All one can say in general is that the keener the competition between the firms of an industry the more likely it is that more labour for the same wage – lower wage costs, in fact – will reduce the prices of the products of that industry. Now, of these industries some produce goods for export. In so far as they do, the prices of their exports fall, and we can expect to export more of them.*

We must conclude, therefore, that harder work by those on time rates† *could* reduce the prices of some of our exports so

---

*The argument is unchanged if prices of goods at home and abroad are rising at, say, three per cent per annum, on the average, and these particular exports rise in price at less than three per cent per annum. For in this case, too, *relative* to other prices at home and abroad, the prices of such exports will decline.

†Those who work harder on piece rates will not, as stated, reduce wage costs, but since the given overheads can be spread over a greater output, the cost per unit in the long run may be lower. The immediate effects on prices, however, can be ignored.

156

inducing foreigners to buy more of them. If foreigners *spent* more money on them than before, the value of our exports would rise, which is of course the effect we are after.* How significant such a campaign could be is a matter for speculation. It is not likely to have a strong appeal for organized labour: and it sounds a note of desperation quite out of proportion with the reality of the situation.

Moreover, it is not a remedy we can depend upon repeatedly. If on each occasion that our imports began to outrun our exports we called for harder work, it would eventually become quite exhausting to comply. If, on the other hand, the measures were treated symmetrically, the government would be obliged to appeal to the nation to work *less* hard whenever exports began to outrun imports.

IV

Yet the main charge against such a 'policy' of harder work is not that it is uncertain in its effect, or that it strikes a ridiculous posture. It is that the desired effect can be achieved much more simply and directly. To illustrate: suppose the exhortation to 'pull up our socks' and work harder were wildly successful, and issued in lower prices for a wide range of exports, two things are simultaneously achieved: first, the country as a whole will have higher 'real' incomes, for money incomes will not have fallen while many prices will be lower than before; and second, British prices as a whole will be lower relative to foreign prices. But it is the second alone that matters for an improvement in the balance of payments.

This can bear emphasis. Achieving higher 'real' incomes does *not* help the balance of payments. At best it is irrelevant. If people want to work harder in order to raise their 'real' incomes,

*The effect on our imports is uncertain. To the extent that people in Britain were a little better off because of the lower prices of some goods, they would buy more imports. To the extent, however, that some of our lower priced goods were substitutes for imports, they would buy fewer imports.

they are at liberty to make arrangements to do so at any time. They do not have to postpone the occasion until an adverse balance of payments occurs. But, in fact, higher 'real' income makes things worse. For of any 'real' increase in our incomes we spend some fraction (about one-fifth) on foreign goods. A rise in 'real' income will therefore cause us to import more, so increasing the trade deficit.

The lowering of British prices *relative* to foreign prices is what matters. But this can be accomplished without any exhortation, indeed without effort, simply by lowering the dollar-price of the pound – by devaluation.* Moreover, since devaluation does not make the pound-price of home-produced goods any lower than before, while it does raise the pound-price in Britain of foreign goods, 'real' incomes in Britain will be reduced. This overall fall in 'real' income acts to reduce our imports (quite apart from the *relative* 'price effect') and therefore also helps the balance of trade.

v

(*iii*) And this incidentally suggests a remedy for balance-of-payments troubles which many economists recommend and which governments up to the present assiduously ignore – not merely devaluation in times of chronic deficit, but freely fluctuating exchange rates.

The mechanism is in principle simple. If at the existing rate of exchange our imports tend to exceed our exports in value, our current demand for dollars will exceed the supply and (in the absence of government intervention) the dollar rises relative to the pound. For example, an excess demand for dollars may cause the dollar-price of the pound to move from $2.40 to $2.00. This automatically starts to correct the adverse balance of payments. To the British public American goods become dearer than before and so we import fewer of them. On the other hand,

* A conceivable alternative to devaluation of, say, twenty per cent in the dollar-price of the pound is a simultaneous across-the-board twenty per cent cut in prices, wages, salaries, rents, etc.

British goods (priced in dollars) become cheaper to Americans, so that we export more of them. Unless the response of consumers on both sides of the Atlantic is very low, our excess demand for dollars (at this lower dollar-price of the pound) will become smaller, or will vanish, or even turn into an excess supply of dollars.

The mechanism of course, works in reverse for an initial excess of our exports: our excess supply of dollar earnings tends to lower the value of the dollar relative to the pound – say from $2.40 offered for £1 to $2.80 – causing us to import more and export less. Thus, in the absence of government intervention to maintain a fixed rate of exchange, the real forces of international trade would be working, via continual movements in the rate of exchange, to maintain equilibrium in the balance of payments.

There can be objections to freely floating exchange rates, and there can be objections to these objections,* the issue of free versus fixed exchange rates being one of the perennial controversies. But as a method of bringing to a close an era of almost hysterical obsession with the balance of payments the possibility of freely floating exchange rates needs to be more actively and more intelligently debated. A great deal has been written about the importance of fixed exchange rates in promoting world trade – and this over a period during which, in the endeavour to maintain fixed parities, international trade has been restricted by increases in tariffs, quotas, controls, subsidies, tied loans and internal deflations. We have been confusing means with ends in another way. A large volume of international trade is only one component in welfare. There are other and perhaps more important components. A high and stable level of employment is one of them. But maintaining a fixed rate of exchange can, and does, conflict with this objective. A flexible exchange rate does not.†

*For a brief treatment of the objections to flexible exchange rates, see Appendix I of my book *Economic Growth: The Price We Pay* (Staples Press).

†An intermediate position is taken up by the advocates of what is sometimes called 'the crawling peg', a scheme that permits governments to alter the exchange rates of their currency continuously though by not more than two per cent over the period of a year. The advantage claimed for this arrange-

VI

There has been one small omission in the discussion which can now be attended to. We have been concentrating on the various methods by which domestic consumers can be induced to buy fewer foreign goods, and by which foreigners can be induced to buy more home goods – this latter being the harder task. If, for example, Britain devalues the pound, from \$2.40 to \$2.00, the goods we import from the United States will cost us twenty per cent more (or $\dfrac{\$2.40,}{\$2.00}$ equals 1.2 times as much as before). If the British buying public's demand for American (and other foreign) goods is sufficiently responsive, some part of its aggregate pound *expenditure* will be switched from the purchase of the now dearer American (and other foreign) goods to the purchase of domestically produced goods. In addition to this home demand for more British goods there will be an increased demand for British goods by Americans (and other foreigners) since British goods are now cheaper in terms of these foreign currencies. In consequence the total pound value of the demand for British-

---

ment is that it prevents speculation. If, for example, Britain is devaluing the pound, in terms of all other currencies, at the maximum allowable rate of two per cent per annum, at the same time that Germany is raising the value of the deutschmark, in terms of all other currencies, at the same rate, then the worth of the pound in terms of deutschmarks would be falling by about four per cent per annum. But even if everyone knows that this policy is being pursued by the two countries there can be no advantage in initially exchanging pounds for deutschmarks with the intention of re-selling them for pounds later *provided* the rate of interest earned on pound balances in Britain (or on British short-term securities) is four per cent per annum above that earned on deutschmark balances in Germany (or on German short-term securities). For the potential speculative gain of four per cent per annum – from exchanging pounds for deutschmarks now and buying back pounds a year later – is exactly offset by the four per cent additional annual interest that is forgone by holding deutschmarks rather than sterling.

The trouble with this otherwise plausible scheme is that it requires a high degree of interest-rate cooperation between countries which may be difficult to arrange if the *internal* conditions in each country call for interest rates that are different from those appropriate to the required interest-rate differential.

produced goods increases. But if Britain is already working to full capacity, or very close to full capacity, this additional demand for British goods – both by the British and the foreign buying public – could not be met unless there was some countervailing reduction in the demand for British goods. If such a counter-vailing reduction of domestic demand for British goods could not be engineered, total demand would exceed capacity and British prices would tend to rise. If our pound rose by one-fifth, then at the new rate of exchange ($2.00 to the pound) they would be no cheaper than before to the foreigner, and we should be back to our pre-devaluation position. All the trade benefit of devalu-ation would have been lost.

It follows that if devaluation takes place in a near-fully employed economy, the government may have to intervene in order to offset the increase in demand for domestically produced goods. Again, however, we must keep a sense of proportion. The net reduction of total domestic expenditure, in order to meet the additional demand for our goods, is not likely to be much greater than one or two per cent of gross national product. It may be accomplished by encouraging a rise in interest rates, or by directly withdrawing purchasing power through additional taxes and/or reduced government spending.

VII

There remains, of course, the political problem of persuading the public to accept such measures. A government can run into difficulties if people entertain expectations of a rise in 'real' income above those that can be realized. This happens to be the case in many countries including Britain. Governments and opposition parties since the war have gone out of their way to create a hypersensitivity to comparative 'real' standards, and to galvanize expectations of continuously rising 'real' incomes. The talk is invariably not only of the desirability but of the *need* for faster economic growth which is repeatedly alleged – without any acceptable economic evidence* – to be quite practicable if

* See Chapter 19.

we, as a nation, would only (as a member of the Royal Family has so graciously put it) 'pull our finger out'.

The persistent inflationary pressures since the war – whether or not accompanied by balance-of-payments troubles – can be attributed in part to political or social causes. In this feverish atmosphere of expectations it has become respectable for all groups – white-collar workers, professional groups, academics, civil servants – to be continually 'on the grab'. Alas, the concessions they collectively wring from the economy exceed the physical productive capacity of the economy. The inevitable consequence is a chronic 'wage-push' inflation.*

Regardless of the causes of the post-war inflation, a number of remedies to combat it have been proposed by economists. They include higher productivity,† a lower level of aggregate employment,‡ a more uncompromising use of monetary policy,§ and stronger government control of trade unions.‖

To conclude, harder work is certainly not *the* remedy for a balance-of-payments deficit; indeed, it is probably the least efficacious method of restoring balance. Harder work, if it were accompanied by a little self-denial (in the form of a renunciation for a while of wage and salary claims) could help to reduce inflation. But this is *not* the same thing as saying that increased productivity *per se* will reduce inflation, which belief is held to be fallacious.¶

* See Chapter 3.
† See Chapter 19.
‡ See F. W. Paish, 'How The Economy Works', *Lloyds Bank Review*, April 1968.
§ See M. Friedman, *Capitalism and Freedom* (University of Chicago Press), especially Chapter 3.
‖ See L. M. Lachman, 'The Causes and Consequences of the Inflation of our Time', *South African Journal of Economics*, December 1967
¶ See Chapter 19.

13   A Large Home Market Helps Exports

'Only by having a large home market can an
industry compete successfully in world markets?'

I

As a generalization this statement is invalid. It cannot, for instance, hold for those agricultural or extractive industries whose average costs of production tend to rise as their outputs expand. In such industries the greater is the total domestic demand the higher are the per unit costs in meeting domestic demand alone and the less, therefore, are such industries able to meet competition on the world market. At best, then, the statement can refer only to those industries that, on balance, enjoy significant economies of large-scale production. Such an industry operating, say, in the U.S. caters to a large domestic market, and produces a large volume of output at low cost. Compared with the same industry operating in Britain it could have a significant cost advantage. It might then be concluded that the U.S. is far more competitively placed for exporting to third markets.

Before sorting this out, the reader is reminded that there is also a question of fact involved. How many industries are there for which a home market of more than fifty million people disposing of a total annual expenditure of some £30,000 million – to say nothing of its existing export markets – is too small to enable them to exploit the full economies of large-scale production? Possibly supersonic aircraft, possibly elaborate computers: what data we have at our disposal are inconclusive on such questions. What we do know, however, is that countries as small as Sweden, Canada, Switzerland, Holland, having a much smaller population and G.N.P. than Britain, manage to compete effectively in world markets in a wide range of highly sophisticated machinery and manufactures. And though there are, admittedly, a great variety of British firms that believe they could lower their unit costs by producing in greater volume, this does not indicate a home market that is too small.

Quite the contrary, it is often the case that the British home market is being shared by a large number of competing firms selling goods that are differentiated in only minor respects. Such firms frequently engage in highly competitive advertising and aggressive salesmanship in a bid to extend their share of the total market for such products. This sets limits to their sales and may well prevent any one of them producing in sufficient volume to make the installation of cost-reducing machinery worth while. One might believe that in such instances an expansion of the domestic market might enable each firm to produce more and possibly, therefore, to lower its average costs of production. Yet it is just because of the competitive nature of such industries that any initial profitable expansion of the individual firm itself tends to attract new firms into the industry. The result is that each firm will end up producing much the same volume of such goods as before and (in the absence of technical progress) at much the same costs.* In such cases as these it is possible to sacrifice variety that may in any case be spurious (in the sense that it could not be maintained if accurate information were readily available to the public)† for lower costs either through government intervention to introduce greater standardization of product or by voluntary agreement among firms to produce only a limited number of distinct qualities or models. The economies of scale that are realized when a much larger volume of each of a smaller number of models is produced by a single plant may then be seen to require a market no greater than, and possibly a good deal smaller than, the existing home market.

II

However, we should not want to evade this issue by taking refuge in a mere absence of facts. If there are no exportable

---

*Technological progress will reduce unit costs of production over time whether markets are expanding or not. But such cost reductions may not be wholly passed on to the consumer because of the advertising expenses incurred in attempting to maintain and expand the firm's market share.

† See Chapter 9.

products today with potential economies of scale that are held back by the limited size of the domestic market there may be such industries tomorrow. We cannot rule out the possibility, so we may as well examine the implications.

To simplify matters we will choose a monopoly industry as a hypothetical illustration. We can fix our ideas further by imagining a single giant industry in Britain producing one type of sewing machine, and a single giant industry in the U.S. producing exactly the same type of sewing machine.* The state of technology is such that for any range of output the greater the volume of production the lower is the cost of the sewing machine – at least after a lapse of time necessary to install cost-reducing machinery.

The British market, we suppose, can absorb 100,000 of these sewing machines a year at the price set by the British firm. The American market, let us suppose, currently absorbs ten times that number at half the cost. All the other countries of the world, none of which produces sewing machines of this type, provide a market for at least a million such machines at the lower American price, or alternatively for about half a million of the same sewing machines when priced at the British figure. But the American firm *already* offers its machine at half the price of the British firm. Since we assumed only one type of sewing machine all the orders would be for the American product. Britain would apparently be unable to compete in world markets. Indeed, unless high enough tariffs were imposed on British imports of sewing machines, the American sewing machine would undersell the British product in its own domestic market. But once American sewing machines began to sell in world markets their costs would become yet lower, and the prospect for British sales abroad apparently quite hopeless.

However, there is an implicit premiss here about the sequence of events. The story is assumed to start at some given point in

* There may be attempts of the two giant firms to compete in other ways, such as servicing the product. They may advertise extensively and differentiate their products in the hope of creating in the minds of a large number of buyers a preference for their product. But the broad conclusions would not be altered by making allowance for these things.

time with each country selling to its own domestic market, but not abroad. Then, as if at a prearranged signal, the two giant firms start scrambling for export opportunities. In that case America is obviously successful since to start with her costs are half those of the British. And the differential gets wider as America starts producing more for third markets. But this peculiar temporal scheme can be defended neither by economic logic nor by an appeal to history. If we allow that the sewing machine industry could have begun in either country, the advantage in this respect moves to the country in which the industry is first established. If the industry happened to start in Britain, the story might open with Britain selling a total of three million sewing machines, and at a third of the cost that would correspond to the production of a mere 100,000 machines. Of this three million, we can suppose further, 200,000 are bought by Britain, 1,200,000 by America, and the remainder, 1,600,000 by all the other countries. With this total volume of production, unit costs are well below those which can be reached by the U.S. alone if that country now attempts to produce entirely for its own needs. By setting up a tariff against British sewing machines, and subtracting its annual purchases from Britain of 1,200,000 sewing machines, America will cause British costs to rise. But British costs will still be lower than American costs, since Britain's remaining sales are larger than the American domestic sales alone (say, 1,000,000 sewing macines). With a far smaller domestic market than the Americans', Britain's costs are still too low for the Americans to compete in third markets.

III

Whether Britain or America has captured world markets, this situation is not likely to continue for long. Even if Britain had already penetrated every market, a technical innovation in some other country, say France, might tempt her to set up a sewing-machine industry in the belief that if, by initially quoting a price below the British price – indeed below its own current costs of production – she could capture world markets. If the French firm were successful, the volume of its production of sewing machines would be large enough to bring costs down to the price initially quoted. Certainly some financial strength would be necessary to sustain initial losses. But a calculation of the expected period of loss and the expected period of commercial dominance might suggest this strategy as a profitable one to pursue. Again, however, following some further technical innovation, another country might make a similar bid for the world market, though it would obviously be resisted by the existing dominant firm. We must conclude that industries which can meet world demand at decreasing unit costs result in *unstable* situations, and the owners of such firms and their employees would not feel very secure.

If technology were like that, however, we should not be surprised to discover that these giant firms, reluctant to expose themselves to such hazards, would come to some agreement by dividing the world market among themselves. In this example, a first agreement might have directed the British firm to provide the sewing-machine requirements of Britain and a large number of other countries, the American firm meeting its own requirements and those of the remaining countries. Alternatively, the giant American engineering firm might agree not to compete outside the American market with sewing machines provided its British counterpart undertook not to sell any washing machines outside Britain. France, Germany, Japan, and other countries able to compete, may also be party to such agreements which can be made more binding by some financial interest in, and possibly financial control of, one or more countries' giant firms, by the firms of some or all of the other countries.

The arguments put forward so far seem to suggest that in relation to opportunities for capturing the world market Britain is no less advantageously placed than the U.S., and in any international agreement her bargaining power would be as strong. But in a world where international trade is regulated by tariffs, quotas and other controls, the U.S. has the advantage of having

167

the largest domestic market. If the U.S. raises a prohibitive tariff against British sewing machines, the annual loss to British exports, we shall suppose again, would be that of 1,200,000 sewing machines. If, instead, the U.S. had captured world markets to start with, the erection of an effective tariff by the British would result in a loss of American exports that is but a fraction of that number. Thus the process of readjustment in Britain following American import controls would be more severe than that in America following a British prohibition of American sewing machines. Moreover, if both countries protected their home markets against each other to start with and sought sales in third countries, Britain's maximum potential sales (domestic and foreign) would be smaller than America's maximum potential sales inasmuch as America's protected home market is larger than Britain's protected home market. In an all-out competition between the two giant firms for the markets of the rest of the world the American one could be sure of the ultimate cost advantage. Provided its financial power was no less than that of its British counterpart, its much larger protected home market would ensure its eventual success – though again we must remind ourselves that in a world of rapid technological innovation such success is ephemeral.

The risk of tariffs or quotas being raised is of course a political one depending on the control of executive power and of the organized representation of producers' and consumers' interests.

IV

What emerges from this discussion is that the proposition about the need for a large home market, at least where the manufacture of the item in question is subject to decreasing cost, is not in itself true. It would not be true at all in a world of unimpeded international trade. In such a world the size of the home market carries no advantage whatsoever. The country which happens to be first in the field enjoys all the cost advantages of large-scale

168

production. Nevertheless rapid technological change plus financial power would give rise to an unstable situation in which first one and then another country could make a bid to undersell the existing supplier country. Such unstable situations, however, would be fraught with risk to competing firms and would be likely to result in international market-sharing agreements.* Even in the world of tariffs, quotas and other controls on international trade, such risks are present in some degree and encourage arrangements between large firms to share the world market. Here the country with the largest protected home market has bargaining advantages. Its unit costs for its protected home market are lower than those in other competitor countries. And the additional requirements of the rest of the world, *less* those of the protected home markets of competitor countries, would still provide a market greater than those of the latter, so maintaining its cost advantage if it came to ruthless competition.

If such technical conditions tend to become marked over the future – if, that is, important internationally traded goods reveal significant economies but only to very large-scale production – several courses are open to potential competitor countries. Working through international organizations such as GATT, the governments of potential competitor countries might make the attempt to keep open the opportunity for any country to capture the world market. But this may not be politically feasible. Alternatively, international agreements, sanctioned by governments, could be reached whereby the sole rights of production of each of a total number of such economies-of-scale items were allocated, initially, among the more economically advanced countries subject to a variety of safeguards. If neither kind of international agreement could be reached or maintained for long, a country such as Britain could opt out of the competition for world markets in such items, importing them from other countries. As such items fell in price over time it could always ensure a movement of the terms of trade in its favour (a reduction in the overall price of its imports relative to the prices of its

* Market-sharing agreements between giant firms in the Common Market countries provide ample evidence for this conclusion.

169

home-produced goods) by employing, if necessary, a quota system in order to ensure that less than before is *spent* on those items whose prices have fallen.*

*Such a quota is quite consistent with a larger volume of imports than before. If, for example, American computers fell in price by twenty per cent, we could import up to twenty-five per cent more computers without increasing our expenditure on them.

14 Britain Would Reap Economic Benefits from Joining a European Customs Union

'By joining a European Economic Customs Union Britain would enjoy substantial economic benefits.'

I

Since many of those who support this view readily grant that the more immediate effects of such an economic union might well be adverse – raising the prices of imported foodstuffs, for instance, and also therefore the cost of living, thereby placing further strains on our balance of payments – we shall ignore short-term problems of adjustment that will face British industry, and government departments, so as to have more time to examine critically the nature of the longer-term economic benefits which, we are told, we shall gain if we join the customs union.

The economic benefits that may be expected seem to be four in number. First, it is said that we, together with the other countries, should gain from the increase in specialization within the area of the customs union. Secondly, by producing for this immensely larger market, we should reap the benefits of really large-scale production. The third advantage is that, once we open our doors to increased competition, our industries would become far more efficient. Fourthly, our wealth would grow much faster if we could only throw in our lot with the more rapidly expanding countries of Western Europe.

If Britain were to gain all these advantages from joining they would certainly add up to a splendid vision of things rapidly becoming bigger and better. However, the broad effect of our joining such a union would be to redirect our trade from other countries – from the Commonwealth also, if no special arrangements are made between it and the new union – towards Europe. There might, indeed, be some growth in the volume of our foreign trade. Whether Britain would gain or lose, however, does not depend on the change in the volume of trade alone: it depends also on the 'terms of trade' – on the price of our imports in terms of our exports.

171

Before going further, however, let us dispose of a common fallacy. It is that the potential gains from our joining a European Union are to be measured in terms of potential reduction in the prices we pay for goods from European countries. We are told, for example, that a German camera costing £26 today would, if we were admitted into the European Customs Union, cost the British consumer only £17. But the fact is that the German camera even now costs this country only £17. If the British consumer pays £26 for it, it is only because the British government levies a tax of £9 on it – that is, the government gains the £9, whereas it is the consumer who would get the £9 if the tax were removed. We could, of course, remove the tariff on German cameras, or on any variety of goods, without joining in any customs union with the country which made them – although a government determined to maintain its revenue from taxes would then have to impose taxes on other goods, or on income.

If we did remove all our tariffs unilaterally, so that our demand for foreign goods expanded unilaterally, our imports, in real terms, would eventually cost us more than they used to. For, sooner or later, we should have to lower our prices in relation to foreign prices (for instance, by devaluation) in order to export enough to pay for these additional imports. But if, instead, Britain were to negotiate reciprocal agreements with these other countries, our exports would also expand, though possibly not as much as our imports. Such a plan of mutual tariff concessions between countries is the exact procedure proposed by a European Customs Union. And it should be made plain from the start that there is no presumption that Britain would gain from the changed pattern of trade. No one knows how much we should lose by buying expensively from these new sources what we had previously bought from our cheap traditional markets.

If both we and the Australians had maintained high tariff walls against each other and also against all other countries, and if Britain were then to form a customs union with Australia, the case would be simple. Australia has an abundance of land compared with Britain, and the gains from Britain's specializing chiefly in

172

manufactured goods and from Australia's specializing chiefly in food products would be substantial. If both countries continued to maintain a high external tariff against the rest of the world, trade with the rest of the world would not change. But there would be an increase in trade between Britain and Australia which could be regarded as highly beneficial to both. For their economies are complementary: Britain produces manufactures and machinery very much cheaper than Australia, these goods being exchanged for wheat and wool which Australia produces much more cheaply than Britain.

In contrast, the increase in trade that would follow our entry into Europe would not be of this sort. A large part of the additional trade we might do with the countries of such a union would be composed of goods which are close substitutes. We should both import and export motor-cars, textiles, machinery, ships and so forth. Furthermore, of the remainder of our increased trade with them, much the greater part would consist of goods we were forced, because of the common tariff wall, to buy from them instead of from more efficient sources of supply, such as the United States and the Commonwealth. In that event, part of our increase in trade with the European Union would simply be the result of French and Dutch butter replacing New Zealand butter, French wheat replacing Canadian wheat, and so on.

II

The calculation of gains and losses is difficult. Not only because the relevant figures are hard to find (in any event there must be plenty of guess-work about the new pattern of trade). Even if, by some sort of miracle, we were to have all the relevant statistics given to us from a divine source we should not know quite what to do with them. Economists have no generally acceptable apparatus through which they can feed the relevant data and extract all the right answers. Economists do attempt to calculate these things, but the results are unsatisfactory for a number of reasons.

First, the value of our gain from a reduction of the tariff on a particular commodity, steel for instance, is measured roughly by multiplying the additional tons of steel imported by half the tariff reduction per ton. This technique, as a rough and ready guide, is reliable enough if the tariff is lowered for only one commodity. When it is applied over a wide range of commodities, and the gains so estimated added together, the result is likely to be a figure that very much exaggerates the total gain.

Secondly, any calculations of gains or losses from joining such a Union ignore divergencies between private and social benefit. It might, for instance, be foreseen that British agriculture would eventually have to contract because, relative to other countries in the customs union, its current costs were high. But this would be to ignore the fact that, on the whole, people in this somewhat over-crowded island may prefer more farmland to more factory sites, more fresh air to more factory smoke, more green space to more towns and cities. The farm subsidies in Britain do, in fact, take account of such social benefits which the existence of certain occupations confers on society. The estimates made of the gains from joining a common market, however, take no account of occasional important differences between the price of a good and its social value to the community.*

Thirdly, any calculation of the economic advantages or disadvantages of joining a customs union must consider the redistribution of income and wealth between different groups within the country. We do not pretend to have any clear notion of what direction they would take; whether, as some suggest, the standard of British workers would fall because of the increased import of labour-intensive goods or because of the large-scale immigration of foreign labour. But this important matter has so far been explicitly disregarded in all the estimates made.

Finally, the estimates that have been made are in the main directed to a different question than the one we are primarily concerned with. The crucial estimate for Britain is that of the gain, or loss, to Britain alone if she elects to stay *out* of a customs

* See Chapter 6.

174

union that has already been formed by the several European countries; whereas the estimates that have been made are of the combined gain, or loss, to a union of such countries that would include Britain. It is more than just possible that a union of such countries which included Britain could boast some net gain for the union as a whole while, at the same time, Britain would become worse off for the venture.

In view of the large margin of error involved in such calculations, a presumption that Britain should join such a European union could be established only if the estimate of gains were overwhelmingly large. Since, in fact, what estimates have been made indicate that the gains are trivial and uncertain, there can be no presumption in favour of Britain's entry. It has been calculated, for instance, that the once-for-all net gains from specialization within a common market that included Britain would be roughly equivalent in value to less than one-twentieth of one per cent of the total output of the seven countries involved. It is also alleged that the 'terms of trade' of this common market of seven countries would improve *vis-à-vis* the rest of the world – their imports becoming somewhat cheaper compared with their export prices. But even this does not bring the total benefits up to one per cent of the value of their combined national outputs.

III

But what of the economies of large-scale production? What would Britain gain through a reduction of costs brought about by large-scale production in such a customs union? Again we know surprisingly little. Some industries seem, at first sight, to promise large economies of scale. But the fall in cost per unit as output expands can also be attributed to increasing experience, to innovation, and to the discovery of cheaper sources of raw materials.

Country-by-country comparisons do not lead us far. Too many factors may be invoked to explain differences in productivity as between the United States and Western Europe, without the size of the market really having anything to do with them.

175

Indeed, if the size of the domestic market is a decisive factor, why is it that small countries like Sweden and Switzerland have so high a standard of living – higher, indeed, than that of this country? It is hard to believe that there are big opportunities for cost-reduction which cannot be exploited in our densely populated home market of over 55,000,000 people, to say nothing of our overseas markets.

IV

Turning to the alleged salutary effects of greater competition from abroad, the first thing to understand is that the experience of greater foreign competition would not be felt over the whole of British industry. In the production of some goods, chemicals, motor-cars, certain machine tools, it would. But in many of those products we currently export to the United States the going would be easier. What is more to the point, however, one cannot infer that increased competition from abroad necessarily increases the efficiency of domestic industry. Efficiency is an ambiguous term in this connection. It could mean business efficiency or it could mean economic efficiency. When journalists and commentators roam about Britain, interviewing industrialists, managers, engineers, designers, foremen and workers about their jobs, and conclude, invariably, that British industry is sluggish, they are talking of incompetence in the methods of production, administration, and selling. While this is important, overall economic efficiency also takes into account the things a country is best fitted to produce for the international market – best fitted as a consequence of its natural resources, its climate, its inherited skills, and its accumulated experience and capital.

To bring out the difference, let us suppose grape-growers in this country were competent, up-to-date, and industrious. For all that, the production of grapes and wine in this country would be – economically speaking – inefficient compared with production in Spain, southern France, or Italy, even though in such areas there might be slackness of effort and an addiction to the old ways of doing things. The removal of our tariff on the grapes

176

and wines of these areas would result in an expansion of their produce – and in a contraction of ours. Overall economic efficiency would be increased, but an efficient industry by business standards would disappear in Britain.

The converse is equally likely, and indeed can be illustrated by the same example seen from within the economies of France and Italy. The inefficiently managed wine industries of Italy and southern France would expand on Britain's joining the Common Market, so extending in those countries the area of business inefficiency. To illustrate further, it seems likely that the British motor-car industry, the watch and clock industry, the iron and steel industry, the glass industry, and industries producing scientific instruments, would on balance have to contract. There is no reason to suppose, however, that as a necessary consequence they would become better organized. Nor can we anticipate that the area of inefficiency, in industry as a whole, might contract unless we suppose – which has not been alleged – that these industries are among the less well managed. Again our sales of aircraft, of woollen fabrics, and of Scotch whisky to other members of the customs union would be likely to expand. If on balance these industries grew larger (there is no assurance that this *will* happen since Commonwealth and other overseas markets are likely to reduce purchases of British goods once we adopt the Common Market tariff against their goods) are we to assume they will become more efficient? Is it possible to argue, and if so on what grounds, that whether an industry expands or contracts in response to market forces it is sure to become more efficient in business terms? In sum, although a larger common market, if it remains competitive, *may* increase *economic* efficiency as a whole (in the sense of achieving net gains for the common market countries taken together) it does not necessarily promote *business* efficiency as alleged; it might well do the reverse.

It is, incidentally, in connection with the future of such industries as those producing aircraft, electronics and computers that much is made of the 'need' for wider European markets in order to support our 'science-based' industries, and of the fears of 'American domination'.* These popular emotional appeals seem to overlook two rather obvious points: first, if a European customs union embracing Britain were in fact required to reap the full economies of large-scale production, it is doubtful whether such industries would tend to be centred on these islands rather than on the Continent. Second, if it is at present cheaper for Britain, and for other European countries, to import certain types of 'hardware' from America than to produce them domestically, cheaper also to import some new technologies than to create them, then there are manifest gains to be made in availing ourselves of the cheaper source of supply.† Profitable international exchange is quite consistent with the sort of 'economic domination' that takes the form of importing goods from other countries which for one reason or another can produce them cheaper than we do – even if the goods in question consist of industrial machinery, computers and aircraft. If, on the other hand, the British public is really concerned that its domestic industry be less restrictive, a far surer way of achieving this is to apply more drastic action to restrictive agreements and to monopoly practices than is within the present powers of the Restrictive Practices Court and the Monopolies Commission.‡

V

Finally, what of economic growth? The present rate of growth in Britain has lagged behind that of other European countries. Of

---

* See Chapters 10 and 13.

† We ignore here the 'infant industry' argument for protecting an economically inefficient industry that promises, over time, to become efficient enough to compete in world markets. We do so for the simple reason that it has not been seriously advanced. If there were reasonable expectations that any Common Market industry, initially protected against world competition, would eventually be able to stand on its own feet, it would be worth-while conducting a cost-benefit enquiry into the matter.

‡ Though Article 85 of the Rome Treaty bolts the front door against price agreements and market-sharing schemes, they can be allowed to slip in by the back door if they masquerade under appropriate euphemisms. Indeed, something of this sort has already begun to happen.

178

course, the figures of *per capita* growth can be misleading. Technological backwardness in one or more sectors of the economies of these countries provides greater scope for faster economic growth. But even if we accept these figures as being faithful reflections of material progress, it is difficult to see how by closer trading relations with faster growing countries the germs of growth would be transmitted to the British economy. At all events, no one has yet given any convincing description of the transmitting mechanism. Certainly, a faster rate of growth in this country could hardly be expected to arise from the increased mobility of capital and labour since, if anything, capital might well flow from Britain to northern Italy and to France, while low-paid labour from southern Italy and France might move to Britain.

Nor is there any historical evidence for the view that an extension of the area of free trade promotes economic growth within that area. The industrial capacities of the United States and Germany, both of them high tariff countries until the war, overtook and surpassed the industrial capacity of free-trade Britain between 1870 and 1900. Is it certain that they would have expanded faster if instead they had pursued a policy of free trade during the nineteenth century?

Again, although there have been no impediments to the flow of goods, of capital, or of labour, between the northern and southern States of the United States, the rate of growth of the South has lagged persistently behind that of the northern States.

Nor must we misinterpret the recent economic expansion in Germany, France and Italy, each of which enjoyed a more rapid economic growth before they formed a customs union than after.

VI

This is one of the least satisfactory of the topics discussed in this volume. It is a large question, and because of the many woolly claims put forward by those alleging that greater economic benefits would accrue to Britain, one has to cover a lot of uncertain ground and engage for the most part in rebutting what *appear* to be the arguments. Enough has been said, however, to ensure a verdict of 'case unproven'. To summarize the conclusions reached: the alleged gains from increased specialization turn out to be, at best, insignificant. In view of the size of our domestic market, to say nothing of an expanding Commonwealth market, the belief that significant economies of large-scale production will be denied us until we have access to a European Customs Union is unrealistic. No good argument has yet been invoked to support the view that a larger integrated trading area must necessarily increase business efficiency. Nor, finally, is there any justification, economic or historical, for the belief that closer economic contact with a European Union will tend to stimulate growth in our economy.

Those in favour of economic union occasionally admit to some, or the greater part of the above arguments, only to fall back obstinately on very large gains of an intangible or, better still, 'dynamic' nature in 'the long run'. While they remain intangible and unspecified, no one can gainsay them. And, however interpreted, so long as they are to be realized only in 'the long run' no one will live long enough to disprove them.

Part 4   Migration Fallacies

15 The Country Needs Immigrant Labour

'In view of the shortage of labour, we should
welcome immigrants for the labour they provide.'

I

Imagine ten men on a desert island, all fully occupied in keeping themselves alive. Could a labour shortage arise in that situation? In order to have access to an underground source of spring water they may have to move a boulder, which feat would require at least twelve men. Alternatively, they might like to carry the division of labour further in order to raise their living standards, but no plan to do so could be implemented without at least an additional five men. The first possibility would come under the heading of 'indivisibilities' – at least twelve men are needed for the project: eleven men will not do. The second possibility, the requirement of a greater number of men if average output is to be raised, is a case of 'economies of large-scale production', which terminology explains itself. In either of these cases the existing ten men stand to gain from an addition to their number and, therefore, each has an interest in remedying the 'labour shortage'.

Neither of these forms of labour shortage, however, contributed to the alleged overall labour shortage in Britain in the 1960s. It could, of course, be urged, though it has not been demonstrated, that there are in Britain economies of large-scale production which cannot be tapped unless the working population is increased by, say, fifty per cent. But such allegations were not made in connection with the 'labour shortage'. This latter phenomenon appeared as an excess demand for labour throughout the economy – an overall demand for more labour than is available in the economy as a whole. And the excess demand for labour was, in its turn, derived from an overall excess demand for goods – an excess, that is, in the value of the country's overall demands for goods (at existing prices) above

183

the value of what is being produced in the fully employed economy.

II

It may seem strange to the thoughtful layman that people can be spending money in excess of the value of the output they produce. If the total of incomes earned over a period is identically equal to the net value of output produced, it is clearly possible for people to spend *less* than the whole of their incomes. In that case some of the output will be left unbought: there will be an excess supply of goods on the market. For excess current demand to exist, on the other hand, people have to spend, overall, *more* than the whole of their incomes.

Another possibility is that though they do not spend more than the whole of their incomes, they do demand a combination of goods different from that produced by the economy. In such case there would *not* be an overall excess demand: there would be an excess demand for certain goods and a deficiency of demand for others. And though this also was alleged, we shall confine ourselves for the present to the allegation of an overall excess demand in the economy.

How is it that people can demand more than the value of what they produce – equal always to the total income received? In fact they would *not* be able to do so if total expenditure on current output came only from current incomes. There are, however, extra sources of spending. Purchases of consumer goods and, more important, purchases of new machinery and buildings for industry, come not only from current incomes but from money saved over the past, whether the money is held in currency or (as is more likely) as deposits in the banks. Since the seller of goods has no means of distinguishing payments out of current income from payments out of stocks of money or bank balances, and certainly has no incentive to do so, he will sell to any buyer who meets his price. In addition to these additional sources of spending, there can be expenditure by the government in excess of the taxes it collects. The additional money

184

the government will require in order to spend more than its tax income will be created by the banks.

There can, therefore, be an excess total demand for goods in the economy – that is, at any given level of prices, a demand for goods in excess of the full productive capacity of the economy – and consequently a tendency for prices in general to rise. Such an overall excess demand for goods will be reflected in an excess demand for labour. Just as there will appear to be an overall shortage of goods, there will also appear to be an overall shortage of labour.

Such a situation is often referred to as one of suppressed, or incipient, inflation. For the overall excess demand for goods acts to raise the existing price level. If wages then rise in the same proportion as the price level, the previous real situation is restored at a higher price level (except for fixed-income earners, a group which obviously becomes worse off when prices rise), without much reduction of the excess demand and without, therefore, much check on the tendency of prices to rise.

Now, the management of the economy, and in particular the maintenance of price stability, is ultimately the responsibility of the government which exerts control on the overall level of demand mainly through its control of the budget and through its control of the banking system. In times of rapid change the maintenance of price stability is not easy. The task becomes still less easy if in addition the government seeks to maintain a level of employment above ninety-eight per cent of the total employable labour force* (indeed, at a level where job vacancies exceed the numbers unemployed). But allowances for extenuating circumstances and, possibly, political follies, do not alter the fact that an incipient inflation arising from the excess demand for goods, is indicative of the failure of the government to discharge its responsibility.

In such a context, then, the so-called labour shortage means just that – a failure of the government to control aggregate demand: no more and no less. Indeed, any economy can generate this sort of 'labour shortage', the Chinese economy as well as

* See Chapter 19.

185

the New Zealand economy, simply by adopting economic policies that result in current expenditure exceeding total productive capacity. The diagnosis, of course, suggests the remedy: the adoption of policies that damp down expenditures to an aggregate value that is – at the prevailing level of prices – no greater than full capacity output.

III

Granted that a general 'shortage of labour' is simply a symptom of incipient inflation, *a condition that is quite independent of the size of any conceivable labour force,* one that arises as a result of inept government management, an interesting question still remains: does the import of labour, like the import of goods, contribute to a reduction of the overall excess demand for goods? If so, immigrant labour serves as a substitute for an anti-inflationary policy. For by adding to the supply of domestic labour it tends to reduce the excess demand for labour. It therefore reduces the so-called labour shortage.

Now if immigrant labourers produced goods for the United Kingdom economy and themselves lived only on fresh air and hope then, quite obviously, immigrant labour would succeed in reducing the overall excess demand for goods. For in such a case immigrant labour adds to the total supply of goods without adding anything to the demand for them. But, of course, immigrants do spend some part of their incomes so that they must add to the overall demand for goods. If, for example, they spent the whole of their incomes on domestic goods they would be demanding as much as they were adding to the total product. In that case immigrant labour would appear to make no difference to excess demand. But they do not in fact spend all their income on domestic goods. Some part is spent on imports. And while, in the short run, this will certainly add to the balance-of-payments problems of the country, the expenditure on imports does imply a reduction in the demand for domestic goods. Again, some part of the immigrants' incomes may go in remittances, and some part may be saved for an emergency or for a deposit on a house or on some other durable good. But even if the resulting expenditure on domestic goods were only, say, fifty per cent of their incomes, the absorption of immigrants into the labour force can still give rise to an increase in the demand for capital goods – both industrial capital goods and social capital goods.

If there happens to be a lot of spare industrial capacity, and also a lot of spare house-room in the country, then, for some time, immigrants could be absorbed into the country while adding less to the overall demand than to the supply of goods. Excess demand would then tend to diminish. But if there is, instead, very little unused productive capacity in industry and very little spare social capital, the demand for these capital items – even though the actual production of them is spread over two, three, four, or more years – will, when added to the immigrants' demand for current consumption goods, result in a total immigrant-induced additional current expenditure that exceeds the value of the output they produce

Thus according to recent calculations, for a steady inflow of mass migration into the United Kingdom – say an annual net inflow of 100,000 or more immigrants – we can expect an addition to excess overall demand for about the first ten years or so, thereafter (unless the flow of immigration is rising) a subtraction from excess overall demand.* Contrary to what has been alleged, therefore, immigration on any scale will not, for some years, act to relieve an overall labour shortage. For the first few years at least it will aggravate that shortage and add to the inflationary situation.†

Before passing on to the question of shortages of labour in particular occupations, the reader should bear in mind that even if economic conditions became such that immigrant labour did

*Nevertheless, for about another decade the steady flow of immigrant-induced savings made available to the domestic economy is likely to be more than offset by the rate of accumulation of foreign liabilities.

† The basis for this estimate is to be found in a paper by Dr Needleman and myself, 'Immigration, Excess Aggregate Demand, and the Balance of Payments', *Economica*, May 1966. A popular version of the paper appeared in the July 1966 issue of *Lloyds Bank Review*.

act to reduce overall excess demand we would still be able to reduce such overall excess demand by traditional monetary and fiscal policies. The only justification for a policy of net immigration is the social or political desirability of a larger, and perhaps less homogeneous, population.

IV

It must be recognized that economists are not all agreed on how shortages have arisen, and persisted, in certain of the so-called essential services. It has been alleged that the inflow of Commonwealth immigrants itself aggravated the initial shortage of domestic labour in transport and nursing; once immigrant labourers were accepted in large numbers in these occupations, indigenous workers (it is suggested) began to regard them as 'coloured' occupations. Some of the indigenous workers moved out of the occupations and the normal recruitment from other than immigrant sources became more difficult. Because these occupations became increasingly served by Commonwealth immigrants, a common belief grew up that the immigrants were helping to overcome an acute shortage of labour. Whereas it is alleged that the immigrants themselves act to generate the shortage of indigenous labour that they then make good. Unfortunately, however, the type of statistics at our disposal does not suffice for a careful examination of this allegation.

Assuming, however, that the shortage of labour experienced was quite independent of the numbers of immigrants entering them, the question of what exactly would have happened to the provision of so-called 'essential' services were it not for immigrant labour is obviously difficult to answer. By ignoring the familiar type of economic analysis based on some ideally functioning competitive economy and by invoking, instead, the alleged innovation-resisting capacities of certain sectors of British industry one might advance the view that, in the absence of immigrant labour, already known and commercially feasible labour-saving devices would have been resorted to.

No casual observer of the U.K. economy would find it hard to believe that some cost-reducing labour-saving innovations are fairly readily available but that, either for institutional reasons (peaceful labour–management relations) or because of the force of inertia, they are not adopted. Without some emergency to act as a catalyst these potential sources of efficiency will be ignored for many years. In transport, for instance, it has long been known that worth-while economies could have been made by the employment of one-man buses, by installing coin-operated turnstiles on underground railways, by simplification in fares, and by other labour-saving devices. In hospitals the saving of trained staff by installing patient-monitoring devices in wards is making only very slow headway. It would not be unreasonable to believe that if immigrant labour had not flowed into these occupations, the apparent shortage of indigenous labour might have precipitated an emergency in which the provision of such services could have been met by a change to more efficient, and already known, labour-saving methods.

However, it is not the layman's picture of a shortage of indefinite duration that troubles the economist but rather the rise in prices entailed by a wholly domestic adjustment to the shortage. The question arises: is the immigrant provision of such services at existing prices not preferable to a rise in the price of the services in the absence of immigration?

One may demur on two grounds: the inconclusiveness of this essentially partial consideration and the possible long-run consequences of accepting the implied policy. Consider the latter first. In an advanced economy subject to continual fluctuations of the conditions of demand and supply, shortages appear from time to time and, depending on institutional factors, continue for long or short periods. A policy of encouraging immigration whenever a sectional shortage of labour existed – in effect using external mobility of labour as a substitute for internal mobility – would, because of its obvious asymmetry, result in a continual net inflow of migrant labour. Moreover, any rule that sanctioned the admission of immigrant labour into an industry after the persistence of unfilled vacancies beyond an agreed time period might well lead to increasing friction between management and labour. For such a rule would act to discourage any industry from negotiating increases in pay, or from raising wages in order to attract domestic labour, if, by waiting a little longer, its requirements could be met by immigrant labour at existing wages.

One cannot, of course, be certain that in the absence of immigrant workers the earnings of indigenous workers in transport and in hospitals would have been higher than they are today. But few economists would think such an outcome unlikely.*

Consider next the partiality of the question posed above. To the passenger deprived of a bus or train service, its maintenance at the same price is certainly to be preferred to its withdrawal or to its continuation at a higher price. This preference can be formalized by making estimates of the worth to the passengers of retaining a given service at the existing price rather than abolishing the service or raising its price. It is not a rounded view, however. If we are to reach a conclusion for the indigenous population as a whole we must also take account of the rise in wage-rates necessary to maintain the service, which gives a clear gain to indigenous transport-workers in the absence of immigration.

How one balances the gains to consumers against the losses to indigenous workers without recourse to the abstractions of 'welfare economics' may appear to be a matter of subjective

---

*Mr Callaghan, in a reply to a question in Parliament about work permits, said: 'The issue of [employment vouchers] has been strictly related to the country's economic and social needs.' (*Guardian*, 17 May 1969.) Elaborating, he went on to say that vouchers were now being issued in relation to the application of employers in Birmingham and elsewhere for persons for specified jobs.

It goes without saying (*a*) that employers will obviously prefer immigrant labour (provided they meet no opposition from domestic labour) if it is thought to be cheaper than domestic labour, or if it will save time searching or save money training men for specific tasks, and (*b*) that these 'needs' of industry are contrary to the interests of the labour force. What is good for business is not, as it happens, always good for the country at large. (See Chapter 8.)

judgement. But it is certainly not obvious that the consumer interest should prevail over the interest of employees.*

V

In the really long run in which immigrants have been assimilated and any consequent capital shortages made good, the crucial question to be posed is whether it is believed to be desirable to create, over the future, a larger population in the host country than would emerge from the indigenous population.

On economic grounds alone there are, apparently, no significant advantages of size to be reaped above a population of about five millions – though much, of course, depends upon the geography and natural resources of the area in question. It avails not to point out that the country with the highest productivity per head is the United States with a population of 200 millions without adding that a country as poor as India has a population well over 500 million, or without observing that countries with populations as small as Switzerland or Sweden provide higher 'real' standards of living than do the much larger industrialized countries of France, Britain and Germany. There is no 'optimal' population for the United Kingdom in any tenable sense – though of course businessmen would love to see a rapidly expanding population, whatever its existing size. If the population density were such that people everywhere had to move sideways to get past one another, businessmen would still benefit from a growing population, since this ensures them expanding markets and raises profits and rents relative to wages.†

It is, I believe, economically feasible, given a few years for adjustment, to accommodate 100 million or more in the United

*This aspect is treated formally in a paper by Dr Needleman and myself in *Economia Internazionale*, May 1968, on the long-term economic consequences of net immigration. There we suggest that if the government succeeds in reaching an 'optimal allocation' with and without immigration, the non-immigration solution to any particular shortage is better for the indigenous population as a whole than is the immigration solution.

† See Chapter 8.

Kingdom, though we should be getting in each other's way and on each other's nerves more than we do today. It is equally feasible, and a good deal more comfortable, for the country to support a population of twenty-five million. If we ignore the hopes of businessmen who thrive on the transitional effects of a rising population and ignore also the occasional solemn, albeit inane, utterances of cabinet ministers about the 'social and economic needs' of a somewhat larger population, the size of population to aim for is very much an open question – with greater comfort, more unspoilt country, and cheaper foods and imports thrown on the side of a smaller population. Indeed, with a substantial increase in population we could become dangerously dependent on food supplies in a world where population is multiplying at an unprecedented rate.

It is hard for the economist to say more. If a larger population is believed desirable on 'non-economic' grounds, or desirable subject to some rate-of-inflow limitation, or subject to geographical or vocational requirements; and if it is desired in full awareness of (a) the short-run inflationary effects, (b) the adverse balance-of-payments effects, (c) the adverse effects on amenity, and (d) the long-run tendencies acting to lower wages in relation to profits and rents, the economist has little to add. Though some of the 'non-economic' considerations bearing on the size of populations could be formally classified as 'spillover effects', in practice an estimate of net benefits or losses to the indigenous populations is likely to elude statistical computation. The immigration issue, like the population issue, may then have to be decided by public debate, though preferably one in which the relevant facts and all the likely social and economic consequences are commonly understood.

VI

One of the relevant facts is that Britain, England and Wales in particular, is one of the most heavily populated areas in the world. It is more densely packed with people than either Japan or Belgium. It has nearly twice the population density of Italy and nearly four times that of France. Indeed, excepting the Netherlands, it is easily the most heavily populated area in the world. It is interesting to observe, then, that the countries from which the bulk of Commonwealth citizens have arrived over the last decade, though frequently regarded as overpopulated, have densities well below that in Britain. Both India and Jamaica, for instance, have less than half the number of people per acre than we have in England and Wales. The figure for Pakistan is about one-third of that here.*

Even if there were to be no further increase of population in Britain, the continued increase of traffic and of building associated with increasing *per capita* real income will, in the absence of drastic controls, continue to aggravate congestion in city and suburb and cause deterioration of the countryside. Another relevant fact is that we are living in the new era of 'population explosion'. As present trends go, we shall add another 500 millions in the next five years to the world's already (in 1968) swollen population figure of 3,500 million, the greater part of this number being contributed by the underdeveloped countries.

With the inevitable extension of communications there will follow a growing realization among the economically underprivileged millions of the apparently increasing disparity between their standards and those of ordinary workers in the economically advanced countries. In the absence of government checks to immigration the growing temptation to enter the few prosperous countries still open to them† would be strengthened by private shipping and airline companies which would find it profitable to encourage mass immigration by offering cheap passenger rates and credit facilities. Attempts to accommodate massive

*See *U.N. Demographic Yearbook, 1964.* Tables 1 and 2 give the following densities per square kilometre for 1963: Netherlands 356, England and Wales 312, Belgium 304, Italy 168, France 87, Japan 259, Jamaica 154, India 151, Pakistan 104, North Amercia 10, U.S.S.R. 10, Africa 10, Latin America 11, Australia 1.

†Countries that are vast and prosperous, and have the lowest population densities, Australia, Canada and the U.S.A., are at present closed to non-white Commonwealth immigrants. There is no likelihood of this policy being reversed in the foreseeable future.

immigration, however, would – quite apart from initial economic disturbances – add pace to the indigenous rise in population density and to the forces making for a decline in general physical amenities. Only within the last decade has the general public begun to recognize that living space on this small planet is strictly limited. Inhabitable areas of natural beauty and tranquillity are among the world's scarcest and fastest-disappearing goods. And from the tragic fact that vast and impoverished communities are perilously close to vindicating the Malthusian prophecy, one cannot conclude that this country would materially benefit by offering itself as an economic sanctuary.*

---

*We are not, however, precluded by the above observations from some attempts to ameliorate the economic conditions of poorer countries if we conceive it to be our moral duty to do so. Though proponents of liberal dogma appear reluctant to concede the possibility, a policy may yet be acceptable to the nation without necessarily redounding to its pecuniary advantage. If, therefore, on moral grounds we wish to make some contribution to the well-being of the poorer countries we could make our contribution the more effective by first undertaking a careful examination of the various methods of affording economic relief and giving direct aid as an alternative to the policy of transferring some part of their growing populations to these islands. In addition to making some contribution to their well-being by a further reduction in our tariffs on their exports, and by other schemes directed towards improving their terms of trade, we should want for instance to compare the effects of offering some proportion of our annual capital formation as an alternative to using this same capital formation to provide some given number of their inhabitants with the economic opportunities of living instead in the U.K.

Consideration of distributional implications would seem to favour exporting capital to importing population. We should hardly regard it as fair to earmark the additional capital sent abroad, as an alternative to using this much capital to equip immigrants in the U.K., to be distributed among those families that might otherwise have entered this country. Rather we should want it distributed within the country according to some more acceptable principle of priorities. Moreover, once account is taken of the greater need for capital in poor countries compared with the U.K., as well as the distributional implications just mentioned, it should not be hard to show that, as a method of economic aid to poor countries, the import of a small proportion of their population is economically wasteful as well as ethically unacceptable.

16 On the Growing Brain Drain

'Unless the earnings of scientists and engineers
are raised and better use made of them, the drain
of British talent to America will continue.'

I

With the 'Jones Report' (Cmd 3417) the so-called brain drain made its official debut in the select society of well-established national economic afflictions – a recurring imbalance of payments, a chronic crawling inflation, a faltering growth rate, and an overall slackness in the pulse of economic life. Since the brain drain is a topic that lends itself so admirably to public lament, and fits so agreeably into our post-war mood of national self-depreciation, it might be thought inconsiderate of the author to attempt to damp the spirit of despondency by an appeal to reasoned argument. But if the reader will reflect on the many sources of genuine pessimism already at the public's disposal he will agree that it should be able to reconcile itself to the loss of a bogus one – especially as I have gone out of my way to furnish some gloomy arguments of real value.*

I do not imagine the task of persuading the public not to worry about brain drains and the like will be easy. Current economic myths appear to be able to weather the facts of economic life remarkably well. Over the last few years, for example, and guided by the initiative of government officials and journalists, we have persuaded ourselves that our country is engaged in a 'desperate struggle for economic survival'. If it is true for the country, it is certainly not true for its *inhabitants*. I have not as yet met anybody in Britain who looks, in the remotest degree, like a person engaged in a desperate struggle for survival. Instead we seem to be surrounded by every manifestation of increasing indolence and increasing wealth – in some respects more wealth than we can manage: our towns and cities are glutted with shiny new automobiles, and the growth of juvenile

* See especially Chapters 20 and 21.

self-assertion and delinquency is, if economically based, attributable more to rising affluence than to hardship.

Be that as it may, what has to be added to the public's sense of economic *malaise*, in this instance, are the apparently authoritative pronouncements about a current shortage of scientists and engineers; as usual, one that is 'sure to get worse' unless, somehow, we pull up our socks, or do something equally drastic.

Now a general economic proposition has it that the price of any particular resource that continues in short supply tends to rise – a tendency which acts to encourage additional supplies being put on the market, so restoring equilibrium. The alleged national shortage of scientists and engineers does not, seemingly, belong to this ordinary market species of shortage. For the earnings of scientists and engineers are regarded not as being too high. If anything, they are regarded by the 'Jones Report' as being too low. It is alleged, moreover, that these men are insufficiently appreciated by industry and are often not as gainfully employed as they might be. To the economist these look suspiciously like the symptoms not of shortage but of oversupply. But of course one must not say such things as it offends against many people's deeply religious feelings about the value of science. Besides, it is a fact that the ratio of scientists and engineers to total population is higher in the U.S. than in Britain – if we accept its classifications as being directly comparable with ours, which is doubtful. What follows from this?

As measured by the index, at least, the U.S. offers a higher standard of living to its citizens than does Britain. Are we supposed to infer a causal link from these facts? If so, let us remind ourselves also that the *per capita* growth rate in the U.S. at present does not happen to be one of the fastest among the wealthier countries. If we do not care for this causal link, the reverse relationship might appeal to us. It is certainly more plausible. A higher standard of living offers the wherewithal for more adult education, though not only in engineering and science, but also in the less approved subjects that find their way into the humanities.

Certainly there is little evidence for the view that the substantially higher earnings of engineers and scientists in the U.S. are the result either of what is sometimes called 'a strong demand situation' there, or of the alleged superior performance (more intensive exploitation?) there of scientists and engineers. Indeed, there is no need for speculation about the *causes* of the so-called brain drain of scientists when the relevant fact is universally acknowledged: namely, that the 'real' earnings of practically every kind of worker in the U.S. are much higher than those in Britain. Hairdressers in the northern states of the U.S. earn more than twice their counterparts in this country. So also do shop assistants, garbage collectors, secretaries, policemen, bus-drivers, nurses, garage hands and call girls. And this without, as yet, any evidence of proportionally superior performance. One may reasonably anticipate that as information spreads – and our Sunday papers already carry American advertisements inviting application from skilled and semi-skilled British labourers – the westward flow of all other categories of workers will gather force, provided always that the U.S. government continues to permit it.

But even if the U.S. were ready to receive from this country any number of British workers, and even if they moved in response *only* to pecuniary differentials, we must not suppose that these islands would eventually be denuded of population. As the labour force in Britain declined and became scarcer relative to the land and capital goods remaining in Britain, 'real' wages would rise in this country. And (ignoring obvious modifications of the argument to allow for economic growth) 'real' wages would begin to decline in the U.S. until the difference in 'real' wages between the two countries vanished. The flow of labour between the two countries would cease.

II

Let us now move on to consider the alterations of the argument necessary when only particular categories of workers are allowed to move freely between the two countries. Again we shall ignore the unimportant modification of the argument necessary to deal with the fact that economic growth is taking place in both countries, and begin by imagining a situation during which there is no transatlantic migration whatever. At such a time the U.K. and the U.S. each has an adequate stock of scientists, the real earnings in each country being such that the flow of newly trained scientists serves exactly to replenish the annual retirement of scientists. (Exactly the same remarks apply to engineers, so that we disregard them for the present or lump them together with the scientists.) Once barriers to migration are lifted, and the much higher real earnings in the U.S. become attainable by British scientists, they begin to move west.

As the British *stock* of scientists shrinks, their value to the economy and, therefore, their 'real' earnings rise. In the U.S., on the other hand, where the *stock* of scientists is expanded by the addition of immigrant scientists, 'real' earnings begin to fall. At the same time, however, and in response to the higher 'real' earnings in Britain the annual *output* of newly trained scientists here begins to grow. In the U.S., in contrast, and in response to the lower 'real' earnings there, the annual *output* of new scientists begins to decline. However, if we take the limiting case where migration responds *only* to material advantages the situation will approach an 'equilibrium' (see below) in which 'real' earnings of scientists are about the same in both countries.

When this equilibrium is reached we shall find that there is, each year in Britain, an excess of newly trained scientists over and above the annual replenishment of scientists required to maintain the now smaller British stock. This annual excess creation of new scientists in Britain is, of course, the number emigrating to America. And this number, annually entering the United States, is exactly equal to the annual demand there for the *additional* scientists which are required to make up the deficiency caused by the annual excess of retirements over newly trained scientists. This steady migration of scientists (again ignoring modifications necessary for growing economies) continues to maintain unchanged the resulting stock of scientists in each country.

It would seem then that, contrary to the general impression conveyed to the public, a westward flow of scientists is not a temporary aberration arising from widespread incompetence in British industry.* Nor does the prospect of its continuation warrant any inference of economic disaster. Indeed, in the absence of future barriers to entry of scientists into America, we must resign ourselves to accepting the 'brain drain' as one of the facts of economic life. What is more, it may well grow larger over the future until something like the equilibrium described above is reached.

*Apart from an inferior endowment of resources in Britain – say, less land and capital per person in Britain compared with America – one could attribute the remaining difference in living standards to a relative 'incompetence' in British industry. But a relative incompetence of such magnitude is not to be remedied within the next two or three years. Even if the United States's economy obligingly discontinued its growth until we caught up, it would take us more than a quarter of a century (growing at an average rate of three per cent per annum) to attain the 'real' standards, or *per capita* productive potential, enjoyed today in the United States. In so far, then, as the westward flow of British emigrants continues to respond to differences in 'real' income we must, in the absence of controls by Britain or the U.S., resign ourselves to its continuation over the foreseeable future.

17 On the Economic Loss from the Brain Drain

*'Since a fully trained scientist or engineer is worth
between £1,000 and £3,000 a year, there is an
annual economic loss to this country of between
£1 million and £3 million for every one thousand
emigrating scientists or engineers.'*

I

This impression, conveyed by reports in the Press, is sometimes
magnified by transforming the future annual earnings of a
scientist to a single sum, say £30,000, to indicate his total
capital value to the nation. Such a sum can be regarded as the
value of the locked-in wealth of the scientist inasmuch as, like
any other asset worth about £30,000, it produces a stream of
future annual earnings. If we want to compare like with like we
have to compare the income of scientists with the national income or else the asset value of a scientist's future earnings with
the value of the total assets in the country, i.e. its national
wealth. We shall, therefore, restrict ourselves to estimates of the
annual economic loss arising from emigrating scientists and
engineers, which will then be directly comparable with the
annual national income or with gross national product.

We can simplify the exposition (*a*) by provisionally forgetting
about the role of government in the national economy, and (*b*)
by concerning ourselves, for the present, with the emigration
from Britain of a single scientist, a Mr S. We need pay no
attention to his account of frustrations encountered in Britain,
or to his hopes of more elaborate facilities and wider opportunities. What is relevant is the fact that he gives up his salary of,
say, £2,000 per annum and accepts instead an American salary
of, say, $12,000 per annum, on condition that he contributes
his services thenceforth in the United States.

Now it is clear that the national income of the U.K. falls
by £2,000 and that of the U.S. rises by $12,000. And this simple
fact alone is in the minds of people who use such figures to
represent the direct loss to this country as a result of the brain
drain. But if this were indeed the measure of economic loss, it

200

could easily be made good by 'importing' as many families as are needed, from any other country, to earn £2,000. National income would then be unchanged, and no economic loss suffered. We could, of course, carry the logic of this argument further, and bring in families earning up to £4,000 between them for every scientist earning £2,000 who left our shores. Such a measure would ensure an economic gain for this country. But why stop there? We could double, or treble, the country's national income within a few years by adopting a policy of unrestricted immigration.

It should be manifest, from pushing the logic of this argument around a little, that subtractions from, or additions to, existing national income do not yield a satisfactory measure of economic loss or gain to the country. One obvious reason is that the numbers of people are changing along with the national income. Unless we are ready to believe that a higher national income is something to be preferred to a lower national income *regardless* of the numbers of people involved – so that an increase of Britain's population from fifty-five million to 165 million, with average income being halved, yields a higher total national income than before and is therefore to be preferred to the present situation – we must consider the numbers of people every time. Indeed we shall not obtain a satisfactory index of well-being, of economic gain (or loss), until we specify the particular group of people whose well-being is in question.

In our example, Mr S. alone must be deemed better off inasmuch as he chooses freely to move to the U.S. On leaving Britain he ceases to contribute his services, valued on the market as £2,000 per annum. But – and this is the essence of the matter – he ceases at the same time to consume £2,000 of goods and services produced in Britain.* Since what Mr S. took for himself from the British economy was exactly equal in value to what he contributed to the British economy, the *remaining* population taken together is no worse off when he leaves for America. Nor

---

*We shall assume, though only for the moment, that Mr S. spends the whole of his income on consumer goods.

will anyone in America be any better off when Mr S. consumes there to the full value of his contribution.

II

The argument will now be advanced in four stages: (*a*) by considering a large flow of emigrants from Britain, which requires that we take account of any rise in the 'real' earnings of scientists generally associated with a reduction in the remaining stock of scientists, (*b*) by bringing into the calculus the 'excess taxes' paid by scientists in Britain, (*c*) by taking account of the reduction of imports associated with any reduction of population and (*d*) by removing the simplification of a competitive economy in which the full (marginal) contribution* of the scientist is reflected in his earnings.

(*a*) Granted that a reduction in the numbers of the remaining stock of British scientists raises the value of their (marginal) contribution to the rest of the economy, and therefore their 'real' earnings, we can make some rough calculation of the loss to the population remaining in Britain of a continuous outflow of 1,000 scientists per annum. This loss to the remaining population is defined as equal, over the year, to the loss of the total contribution of the 1,000 scientists to the economy *less* their total 'absorption' from the economy (provisionally assumed to equal their total incomes). This excess contribution, above their absorption, is not likely to be very great. It is certainly very much less than their total earnings which have been used, incorrectly, as a proxy for the economic loss suffered by the country.

Adopting a figure for the earnings of scientists as lying between £1,000 and £3,000, we take as *average* earnings for an emigrating scientist, had he stayed in Britain, £2,000 per annum over the

*The *marginal* contribution of any number of scientists (or of any class of workers for that matter) is the difference to the value of their total contribution made by employing one additional man. *Incremental* contribution of the additional man also conveys the sense.

next thirty years – again, ignoring the general rise in real earnings resulting from economic growth. The total number, or stock, of scientists (including engineers) in Britain, we take to be 250,000. In addition, the calculations require knowledge of a 'coefficient' e, which relates any reduction in the stock of scientists to the resulting rise in their 'real' earnings. In the absence of reliable estimates for e, I follow tradition in arbitrarily adopting a value of unity (which means that a one per cent reduction in the initial stock of scientists raises their (marginal) contribution – and, therefore, the 'real' earnings of each of the remaining scientists, by one per cent).* A glance at Table 1 below will convince the reader that the actual value of this coefficient e may be several times as large, or as small, as the

Table 1. Showing estimates of economic loss to Britain, as defined, of a steady outflow of 1,000 scientists per annum (ignoring adjustments for growth) for e equal to unity (column 2) compared with the usual (incorrect) estimates based on reductions of national income (column 3).

(1)	(2)	(3)
	Net Economic Loss (as defined	*Reduction of National*
Loss for:	*above)*	*Income*
1,000 scientists during year 1	£ 4,000	£ 2,000,000
Additional 1,000 scientists during year 2	8,000	4,000,000
. . . .	. . .	. . . .
. . . .	. .	. . . .
Additional 1,000 scientists during year 30	120,000	60,000,000
Additional 1,000 scientists during year 31 and thereafter	120,000	60,000,000

*If e instead were equal to 2, a two per cent reduction in the stock of scientists would be needed to raise their (marginal) contribution – and, therefore, the 'real' earnings of each of the remaining scientists – by one per cent.

one adopted without effectively diminishing the striking contrast between the estimates of economic loss as defined above
and the usual (incorrect) estimates based on a reduction in
national income.

Column 2 of the table shows that, given an average working
life of thirty years from time of departure, a steady outflow of
1,000 British scientists a year would entail a net loss to the
country of only £4,000 in the first year, £8,000 in the second year,
and so on up to £120,000 in the thirtieth year, at which time a
total of 30,000 scientists would have emigrated from Britain to
the U.S. over the three decades. Thereafter there is a *constant*
annual loss to Britain of £120,000. And this notwithstanding the
continued outflow from Britain of 1,000 scientists a year since,
on average, 1,000 of the 30,000 British scientists in the U.S.
retire each year and are replaced, so maintaining thereafter a
constant stock of 30,000 British scientists in the U.S. – which
clearly implies a permanent reduction of the same number,
30,000, in Britain's domestic stock of scientists.* This figure of
£120,000 per annum (the excess of total contribution over total
'absorption') should be compared with the reduction of
£60,000,000 in U.K. national income, which reduction is
usually and mistakenly regarded as a measure of the economic
loss to the country. Even if our guess for *e* were wildly out – say
it transpired that *e* was as low as 0.1, and that, therefore, our
estimates were only one-tenth of the true figure – the usual
measure of economic loss would still be fifty times too large.

III

(*b*) Let us turn now from this loss arising from the economics
of the problem, to an additional loss arising from the structure
of the tax system. Each family may be thought of as entering
into a compact with the government, paying so much to it as
taxes and receiving in exchange certain government services.
Since the total tax paid by any person rises with his earnings

* See section II of Chapter 16.

while the receipt of government services do not, the poor are net gainers and the rich net losers by this compact. Our scientist, Mr S., has an income well above the average. The excess of his tax payments above the value he receives from governmental activities is therefore a net contribution to the rest of the community. For to this extent he contributes to the economy more than he 'absorbs' from it. When he emigrates, this net contribution to the rest of the community is lost.*

An estimate of this annual excess tax paid by scientists in Britain can be made by following the practice of supposing the average family of a scientist to consist of a couple and two children. By assuming that every person in the population benefits equally from defence, administration of justice, police, etc., and allocating the value of social services with reference to 'The Incidence of Taxes and Social Services Benefits in 1963 and 1964' (Economic Trends, August 1966) one comes up with an average figure for excess tax per scientist of roughly £150 per annum – this being an unweighted average of *minus* £100, £100 and £450, which are rough calculations of the annual amounts of excess tax paid on incomes of £1,000, £2,000 and £3,000 respectively.

Table 2 shows the loss to Britain of excess taxes arising from a

*Now this aspect of the argument has not been wholly ignored. But whatever the estimate of loss of this excess tax it has not been properly related to the estimate of economic loss, however calculated. Moreover, this loss of excess tax has frequently been improperly presented as follows: as a result of emigration into the U.S. the American government is able to tax the high incomes of British scientists, which high incomes are made possible only by the costly investment in education that is financed from *public* revenues. Britain therefore loses the opportunity of recouping by taxation the sums it spends on the training of its emigrating scientists.

This argument is specious. Whether the science student is financed by public funds or by private means of his own, and whether public funds are offered to him as a loan or a gift, he will – once he is employed as a scientist – be paying excess tax in the U.K.; or, for that matter, in any other country he chooses to work in. The loss of this excess tax along with the migrating scientist may legitimately be regarded as an economic loss to Britain and an economic gain to the U.S. But it should be apparent that this 'transfer' of excess tax will take place irrespective of the way in which the migrating scientist financed his training.

steady emigration of 1,000 scientists per annum (ignoring adjustments for economic growth). The first 1,000 scientists to leave involve the exchequer in a loss of £150,000 per annum. If scientists continue to leave at that rate, the peak annual loss of £4½ million per annum will be reached after the thirtieth year, and will continue at that figure thereafter.

The institution of progressive taxation is clearly going to be a very much more important source of loss to the country than the operation of economic forces. Yet even when we add these two types of loss together, and make allowance for a wide margin of error, the total loss bears no comparison with the estimates based on a reduction of national income.

The outflow of scientists was reckoned in 1967 to be at the rate of 6,200 per annum gross. When allowance is made for the inflow into this country (ignoring differences in quality) the net outflow is reduced to about 2,700. Let us take a 'pessimistic' view of the future, however, and suppose that the *net* outflow of scientists will not stabilize itself until it reaches the 10,000 mark, nearly four times the 1967 figure. The peak loss to this country, reached thirty years after this outflow of 10,000 begins, will on these calculations be equal to £46,200,000 per year (£45,000,000 from Table 2 loss, and £1,200,000 from Table 1 loss), or about

Table 2. Showing loss of excess taxes to Britain due to steady outflow of a thousand scientists per annum (ignoring adjustments for growth).

Loss for:

1,000 scientists during year	1	£	150,000
Additional 1,000	2		300,000
. . . .			
. . . .			
Additional 1,000	30		4,500,000
Additional 1,000	31		4,500,000
	and thereafter		

one-twentieth of the annual *increment* of our gross national product, reckoning the average growth rate for Britain to continue between two and three per cent per annum. Moreover this estimate of loss, as a *fraction* of the increment of G.N.P., does not

206

change over the future even when we allow for overall economic growth, provided that the 'real' earnings of scientists benefit from economic growth no more than do the earnings of the rest of the population.

(c) Though perhaps shameful to mention it, there is also, however, a direct source of gain from the emigration of scientists, as indeed from the emigration of any group of people; one arising from the fact that as a nation we spend about a fifth of our income on foreign goods. The emigration of any family with an average income of £2,000 reduces Britain's import bill by about £400. The annual emigration of 1,000 scientists and their families, therefore, saves us £400,000 in imports in the first year, an import-saving that rises to £12,000,000 in the thirtieth year and thereafter. Thus an equilibrium outflow of 10,000 scientists per annum will, after the thirtieth year, be saving the country about £120,000,000 of imports each year.

Now the value of any annual import-saving can be transformed into a gain figure that is commensurable with the losses estimated in the preceding two tables simply by calculating the more favourable 'terms of trade' which would eventually result from this saving of imports. Since more favourable terms of trade may be taken here to mean a reduction in import prices there is an offsetting gain from emigration arising from Britain's being able to buy foreign goods more cheaply than she would be able to do in the absence of emigration. A rough measure of the country's annual offsetting gain is, therefore, equal to the percentage reduction in our import prices (that results eventually from the emigrants' annual import saving) *multiplied by* the total value of our remaining imports. The more sensitive is the volume of foreign trade to changes in the terms of trade the smaller will be this offsetting gain: for then only a small improvement in Britain's terms of trade – a small reduction in import prices relative to domestic prices – would be required to restore the balance of payments. In fact the response of foreign trade is not very sensitive.* By taking coefficients that express a relatively

* Assuming that the balance of payments is to be maintained over a longish period by altering our domestic prices relative to foreign prices,

207

sensitive response we have probably understated the annual gain from import savings per 1,000 emigrating scientists and their families. These gains are presented in Table 3 below.

Table 3. Showing gains from relatively cheaper imports to Britain arising from a steady outflow of 1,000 scientist families per annum (ignoring adjustments for growth), with $m = n = 2.5$.

1,000 families during year 1	£ 90,000
Additional 1,000 2	180,000
. . . .	. .
. . . .	. .
Additional 1,000 30	2,700,000
Additional 1,000 31	2,700,000
and thereafter	

By subtracting the losses from Tables 1 and 2 from the gains in Table 3 we reach the comforting conclusion that there is little loss to the country from an outflow of scientists of the magnitude contemplated. Adding together the results of Tables 1, 2 and 3, gives a net loss per annum for an annual outflow of 10,000 scientists and their families of £640,000 in the first year, building up to a maximum loss after thirty years of less than £20 million – say one fiftieth part of the annual *increment* of G.N.P. These calculations are, admittedly, very rough, but no degree of refinement in them is likely to alter the conclusion that usual figures for economic loss based on the reduction of national income grossly overestimate the loss to the country from the emigration of scientists and engineers.

(*d*) Before ending we must turn briefly to the popular view that the scientist contributes more to society than is reflected in his

---

we require to estimate *m* (the per cent increase in the volume of our *imports* following a one per cent rise in their average price) and *n* (the per per cent increase in the volume of our *exports* following a one per cent rise in their average price). A figure of 2.5 for both *m* and *n* which is adopted here is fairly high. If *m* and/or *n* were below this figure, the gains would be higher than those shown in Table 3.

earnings. This view may be interpreted in at least two different ways: (1) That the total number of scientists, taken as a body, contributes to society a value in excess of their earnings – sometimes believed to be borne out by the argument that, since the emigration of scientists causes a rise in the price of their services, the remaining population as a whole becomes worse off. (2) That an *additional* scientist, on the average, confers benefits on society, the 'true' value of which exceeds his pay; and this either (*a*) because his pay happens to be depressed below what it would be on a free market as a result of state intervention or of some form of industrial monopoly or (*b*) because some of the benefits he bestows on society at large are just not priced on the market.

The first interpretation (1) is the result of confused thinking. Every group cooperating in the production of a good or service is worth more than it receives in the particular sense that if any one group were wholly withdrawn the production process could not continue. For all that, a well-functioning market tends to price the services of any member of a group, say those of a chemical engineer, at a sum equal to the marginal, or incremental, value of such services to the economy. Inasmuch as an increase in the existing numbers of chemical engineers alone, say from 1,000 to 1,200, is accompanied by a reduction in the marginal value of their services, the earnings of each one of them will decline. However, the resulting loss suffered by each of the previous 1,000 chemical engineers (following an expansion in their numbers to 1,200) entails a gain for the rest of the community – that is, the community *minus* all the chemical engineers. For the rest of the community, so defined, the price of chemical engineering services and, therefore, also the prices of chemical products, will fall compared with the prices of all other services and products. The reverse is also true. If the number of chemical engineers falls from 1,000 to 800 the value of their marginal services and, therefore, the earnings of each of the remaining 800 will rise. They will be better off than before but at the expense of the rest of the community which now has to pay more for their services and for the goods they help to produce. But,

209

and this is the crucial point, the whole of the community remaining after the 200 chemical engineers emigrate – that is, the 800 chemical engineers and the 'rest of the community' – is just as well off as it would be if the 800 chemical engineers continued to receive no more than their previous earnings. For this rise in their earnings constitutes nothing more than a *transfer* of 'real' income from the 'rest' of the remaining community to the 800 chemical engineers. The remaining community as a whole is therefore no worse off as a result of this internal transfer of income as between its members.

In the question at issue, therefore, the remaining British population will not be any worse off as a result *per se* of any rise in the pay of the scientists remaining behind. Their rise in pay is, as suggested above, merely a transfer of income to them from the non-scientist rest of the population; the total income of the whole of the remaining population – scientists and non-scientists together – being unchanged.

(2) Turning to the second interpretation, (*a*) is a distinct possibility, though whether it is being alleged that the government is paying scientists salaries below those that prevail in a free market is uncertain. One might infer as much from occasional statements about 'many unsatisfied demands' for scientists in the British economy, though there is no statistical evidence pointing to a shortage of them. Indeed, the repeated allegations that scientists are underpaid, and underemployed, would, if accepted at face value, indicate not a shortage but a *surplus* of scientists. Still, it is always possible that the market is 'misinformed' in so far as businessmen do not fully realize the uses to which scientists may be put. Allegations of slackness and lack of imagination in British industry are always received with enthusiasm, and I should not want to show such poor taste as to insist on evidence. But it goes without saying that, even if such alleged defects of British industrial management are specified, confirmed and eventually overcome, the so-called brain drain will be likely to continue so long as differences between countries include substantial differences in 'real' earnings.

As for (*b*), it is possible that there exist recognizable benefits

210

conferred on society by scientists as a whole and, therefore, also by the marginal scientist which, for institutional reasons, remain unassessed in the economic system. If so there is a case for paying scientists direct subsidies for the uncompensated services they perform. However, no firm evidence supporting this view has so far been adduced.* Indeed, one might have thought that if this were a characteristic peculiar to scientists it would be at least noticeable in the U.S. also. But so far nobody has noticed this. The 'Jones Report', for instance, which appears to regard the U.S. as an impeccable example of efficient organization, and as a model for this country, nowhere suggests that the market price for scientists in the U.S. is too low.

* I have deliberately ignored the satisfaction that the community may derive from the prestige of having a large number of scientists, and the particular dismay it may feel when some eminent man transfers his services to another part of the world. If this consideration is important to the community, it should obviously be taken into account. But those who have sought to estimate the economic loss to Britain of emigrating scientists have not thought it proper to bring it into the calculus. I confined myself therefore to the fallacies in their existing arguments.

Part 5   Fallacies About Economic Growth

18 Faster Economic Growth Helps the Balance of Payments

*'Faster economic growth is the only way of
permanently overcoming our balance-of-payments
deficit.'*

Although statements like this are frequent enough, in the context in which they appear they partake of the nature of exhortation as well as of fact. The writer would probably assert that faster economic growth is not the *only* way of improving the balance of payments, but that it is the *most desirable* method of doing so. Indeed, the prevailing belief seems to be that economic growth is something that will overcome a whole wilderness of problems: problems of employment, of regional development, of stabilization, of industrial relations, of racial conflict, of juvenile delinquency, of defence strategy, of preservation – the list might be extended to cover all problems connected with education, culture, and the good life. We shall, however, resist the temptation to subject some hypothetical 'growthman' to a Socratic inquisition and, instead, confine our attention to a simple and apparently sober proposition: that faster economic growth is *one* way of improving our balance-of-payments position – more precisely, one way of increasing the value of our exports and/or reducing the value of our imports, or, put more generally, of increasing the value of our exports by more than the incidental increase in the value of our imports. If we can show, then, that economic growth *per se* is not likely to improve the balance-of-payments position, the question of preferring this method to others does not arise.

I

If we suppose that the pound will continue to be 'pegged' in terms of other currencies – for instance, that governments have agreed to intervene in the foreign exchange markets so that £1

215

will continue to exchange for $2.40 (subject to a slight allowance either way) – a uniform reduction in all our prices by, say, five per cent will appear as a fall of five per cent in our prices to every other country. Provided that the prices of all traded goods of all other countries do not also fall by as much as five per cent our prices will appear cheaper than some foreign prices. We should then expect that foreigners would turn to buying somewhat less of their own goods, or of the goods of other countries, and to buying more of British goods. Obviously this would increase the volume of our exports. Again, we in this country would switch over to buying more of our own goods and fewer foreign goods, so reducing our imports. Provided that our response is large enough to ensure that we now *spend* fewer pounds on our imports than before, our balance of payments will improve.

Now this fall by five per cent in our prices could be brought about by a rise of productivity over time that exceeds the rise in wage rates over time. If, for example, overall productivity rose by as much as seven per cent per annum and wage rates, on the average, rose by only two per cent per annum, then unit costs and, therefore, prices, would decline by roughly five per cent per annum. This country would then have a competitive advantage over other countries – again, provided similar changes are not taking place elsewhere.

This simple reasoning, however, constitutes no more than a statement of logical possibilities.

If one could bring into being a seven per cent per annum increase in productivity and *if*, at the same time, wage-rate increases occurred at two per cent per annum on the average then it follows 'as night follows day' that product prices would fall at about five per cent per annum.

If, further, foreign prices did not fall – or at least if they did not fall by as much as five per cent per annum – foreigners would wish to buy more of our goods.

If the volume of our goods sold to foreigners exceeded five per cent then the *value* of our exports would rise.

If, finally, we do not start importing more than before as a result of our increased productivity, our balance of payments will improve – always supposing that, in consequence of our trade advantage, foreigners will not persuade their governments to impose tariffs or other controls against our exports. But there are already enough ifs here to peel the generality off any statement.

II

As we shall show in Chapter 19, an *expectation* of steadily rising prices may be one of the more important circumstances favouring a faster rate of economic growth in advanced economies. If this is so, and faster economic growth follows in the wake of rising prices, then these rising domestic prices will tend to reduce the volume of our exports and to raise the volume of our imports (unless foreign prices happen to be rising as fast or faster). As a result of this kind of economic growth, then, there can be a deterioration in our balance of payments.

The possibility of faster economic growth generating faster price rises, a strong possibility, is by itself enough to invalidate the general statement that faster economic growth improves the balance of payments. Nevertheless, in order to give the growth proponents a run for their money, we shall be sporting enough to ignore this possibility entirely and to suppose, instead, that an increase in our rate of economic growth proceeds smoothly. Indeed, we shall be very imaginative, and suppose that the faster rate of economic growth is the direct consequence of the government's eloquent appeals to enlightened self-interest. There is, therefore, no upward pressure on prices. We shall now look briefly at the effects of this higher rate of economic growth, first (1) on the value of our imports and then (2) on the value of our exports.

(1) If, as we now suppose, the higher rate of economic growth does not affect the domestic level of prices compared with prices abroad then it will act to increase the volume, and value, of our imports. Why? Simply because one of the few 'certainties' in economics is the existence of a fairly constant ratio between the volume of imports and the real national income of a country.

This ratio may alter over time, or even shift in response to some change in tastes, or some political factor. But what is significant here is that a rise in real national income (which reflects the average increase in productivity) will lead to *some* rise in imports. An idea of the magnitude involved for Britain can be had by working out the ratio of total imports to national income in recent years. This ratio, commonly referred to as 'the average propensity to import', is now between one-quarter and one-fifth. A £50 million increase in our national income, for example, will induce an increase of imports of at least £10 million. And if real national income, from increasing at the rate of two per cent per annum, were to increase at four per cent per annum, then in each successive year our imports would grow roughly by an additional two per cent of the (growing) national income *times* this average propensity to import. For instance, in the fifth year after this happy 'break-through' of the growth barrier, the value of our imports would be somewhat more than ten per cent again of what they would have been in the absence of any rise in our rate of economic growth.

Irrespective then of the particular innovations that contributed most to the increase in our economic growth, this general connection between real income and imports can be depended upon to stimulate our imports. Against this upward force on our imports, however, we have to place a force working in the reverse direction, one arising from technology. If the innovations being applied in industry enabled us to produce goods that were more competitive with our imports, let us call them import-competing innovations, people in this country would start switching their purchases from foreign goods to domestically produced goods, and this would reduce our imports. Obviously, one cannot predict the outcome of these two opposing influences unless one knows much more about the types of improvement in technology that are expected, and about people's responses to them. Enough has been said, however, to cast doubt on the growth remedy for our balance-of-payments difficulty. And we are afflicted with yet more doubt when we turn to consider the export side of the problem.

Faster Economic Growth Helps the Balance of Payments

(2) There is, alas, no symmetrical 'average propensity to export' which would act to increase the foreign demand for our goods whenever our real national income increased. The appropriate symmetry in this connection is to be found not in our *own* real national income, but in that of the foreigners' real national income. As the aggregate real incomes of foreigners increase, they import more from all countries. These include Britain which therefore exports more to them. But though this is obviously an important factor in the growth of our exports, it is not relevant to our problem: for we are concerned only with those unilateral measures we ourselves can take in order to improve our exports. In particular we are asking whether faster economic growth of this country will contribute to a rise in the value of its exports.

Any increase in the *volume* of our exports, in so far as it is a consequence of faster economic growth, must arise from an improvement in our technology. We have already discussed the effects of import-competing innovations. Some part of our improved technology, however, may have gone into inventing *new* kinds of products which foreigners wish to buy (and in the buying of which they do not reduce, by an equal value, their purchases of other things we export to them). This is all to the good. On the other hand, our improved technology may well take the form of a reduction in the prices of our exports. At any rate this seems to be the feature that growthmen seem to have constantly in mind. But if this is the case, if our export prices do fall – or, at least, fall relative to foreign prices – the outcome is, once more, uncertain. For what counts here is whether, on balance, foreigners *spend* more on our goods. And it is quite possible that, at our reduced prices, they take more of our goods while spending less money on them. And this would reduce the *value* of our exports.

If, for example, the prices of our exports fell by ten per cent and, to take an extreme case first, foreigners bought exactly the same *volume* of our exports as before, they would be spending ten per cent less on our exports. In other words, our export receipts from abroad would decline by ten per cent. If they took a little more than before, but not as much as ten per cent more of our exports, they would still be spending less than before. In fact they would have to take about ten per cent more* of our exports in order for their expenditure on our exports to remain unchanged. Only if, in response to a ten per cent reduction in our export prices, foreigners bought a bit more than ten per cent of our goods would the *value* of our exports to them increase. For some of our export industries, this condition will be met. For others it will not be met. Opinion on the question varies, and that which is voiced most persistently turns out to be based more on doctrinal faith than on reliable empirical studies.

It is no exaggeration to say that economists as yet know very little about the areas in which, if an increase in economic growth were realized, technological improvement would manifest itself. To what extent it would appear in import-competing industries, to what extent in purely domestically consumed goods, and to what extent in exportable goods – and, in the latter category, which of these exportable goods faces a foreign demand that is, on balance, sufficiently elastic† – are, at present, matters of legitimate conjecture but not of fact. The only honest conclusion one can draw from these considerations is that, for an economically advanced country at any rate, there is no general presumption that an increase in the rate of economic growth *per se* will improve its balance of payments.

IV

It is hardly necessary to remark that our conclusion does not constitute an argument against a policy directed towards

* Actually they would have to buy 10/90 more of our exports (or 11.11 per cent more of our exports) to maintain the *value* of our exports to them.

† The foreign demand for a product is defined to be 'elastic' if a one per cent fall in its price induces foreigners to increase their purchases of it by more than one per cent. The demand is 'inelastic' if when its price falls by one per cent they increase their purchases by less than one per cent. As indicated above, unless their demand is elastic, the value of the exports in question will decline.

economic growth. If it is believed that, on balance, economic growth is desirable – though this is by no means self-evident* – the possibility of a higher rate of economic growth aggravating balance-of-payments difficulty need not be regarded as a decisive argument against faster economic growth. No country is so constrained by the policies of other countries as to deprive it entirely of ways of dealing with a resulting deficit in its balance of payments. It may even hope for some sympathy and cooperation in this event.

It may be necessary, however, to add that the above argument does not deny the possibility of discovering figures that reveal, over time, a *positive association* between faster economic growth and an improved balance of payments. The above argument purports to show only that, in general, faster economic growth cannot be said to *cause* an improvement in the balance of payments. The reader must also bear in mind the terms on which the arguments have been developed, especially the conditions of fixed exchange-rates, of unchanged price-levels in other countries, and of our ruling out of order all political and other events, fortuitous to the analysis. A change in any of these conditions, whichever way they act, may have important repercussions on the balance of payments.

Thus, if a country devalues its currency after a rise in the rate of economic growth, *or* if in the other countries price-levels happen to be rising yet faster than in the home country, *or* if new markets are opening up, *or* if import-controls and tariffs are being removed in other countries, *or* if there is a government policy of protecting new industries that compete with imports, *or* if there is a policy of encouraging investment in industries producing import-substitutes, *then* faster economic growth may well be observed to accompany an improved balance of payments. But it would still be true to say that faster economic growth, by and of itself, cannot be depended upon to improve a country's balance of payments.

*See Chapter 21.

19 Faster Economic Growth Checks Inflation

'Faster economic growth is the only way of
combating wage inflation.'

Wage-inflation, sometimes called 'cost-push' inflation, is supposed to originate in the demands by trade unions for higher money wage rates. It is usually juxtaposed to 'demand-pull' inflation, the result of an excess of demand over productive capacity. Under such conditions labour appears 'scarce' at the existing level of wages which is, therefore, bid up by industry. In times of high employment the distinction between 'cost-push' and 'demand-pull' – which seems to turn on which party, organized labour or industry, takes the initiative in raising the price of labour – is not easy to maintain. But this need not trouble us here: the arguments we use could apply to either kind of inflation.* For the purpose of exposition, however, it will be simpler to think of workers taking the initiative.

I

The accent in the quoted statement above need not be on the *only*. If faster economic growth was one among several ways of damping down a country's inflation, but one which was certain of working, it would be a fact worth knowing. Indeed, in that case it would be less worth-while, though still useful, to show that there are yet other ways of fighting inflation. It is very much worth our while, however, to extend our task by showing that faster economic growth cannot be relied on as a cure for inflation.

First, we must note that there is a particular sense in which the statement that increased productivity prevents a rise in prices is

*The reader who is interested in this distinction between cost-push and demand-pull inflation should consult A. J. Hagger, *The Theory of Inflation* Chapter 5.

necessarily true and necessarily trivial. To illustrate, if throughout the country workers demand, on the average, a wage increase of four per cent per annum, the demand could be granted without a rise in unit costs and, therefore, without a rise in prices taking place provided the overall productivity of labour also rose by four per cent per annum. For the four per cent addition to money incomes can be spent on the four per cent addition to output valued at the same prices as before.*

To push this arithmetic a little further. If labour productivity increased by as much as six per cent per annum, an annual all-round wage increase of four per cent per annum would allow an annual *fall* in prices of about two per cent. For an addition of six per cent to labour productitivity implies, roughly, that six per cent less labour is required to produce any good. If the price of labour were unchanged the wage-cost of any such good would then fall by six per cent. But if, as we have supposed, labour now costs four per cent more than before, the wage-cost of goods will fall by only two per cent. In contrast, if productivity rose by no more than two per cent per annum while wage rates rose by six per cent, wage-costs of goods would rise by about four per cent per annum. It would seem that the stability of wage-costs, and therefore (over a short period) of prices, requires that average productivity and wage rates move upward together through time.

A modification of this conclusion is necessary before going on. A large proportion of the workers in any country is unable to show any significant increase in productivity over time, owing to the nature of their occupation. These occupations simply do

*The increase in overall productivity may well arise not only from the additional efforts of labour but from additional capital, from technical innovation, from reorganization or increased managerial efficiency. Whatever the combination of factors responsible for the increased output a smoothly working competitive market will tend to redistribute the total product by reference to the resulting *marginal* (or incremental) products of each of the groups of cooperating agents in the productive process. We have chosen to ignore this source of complexity – which, if allowed for, would not in any case alter the conclusions – by supposing that any increase in output is available to be divided among the whole of the working population.

not lend themselves to technical innovation. One thinks, in this connection, of the performing arts, of teachers, civil servants, soldiers, policemen, hairdressers, hostesses, bus- and train-drivers, servants, shop assistants, office staff, and so on. If, taken together, the value of their services amounted to fifty per cent of the national output, with industry (including agriculture and mining) accounting for the other fifty per cent, any overall increase in industrial output alone of five per cent would imply no more than an average of $2\frac{1}{2}$ per cent increase in output for the economy as a whole – for we are supposing the 'services group' has a zero increase in real output. Put otherwise, in this 'fifty-fifty economy' an average increase of five per cent in industrial output per man hour implies an average increase of $2\frac{1}{2}$ per cent in output per man hour for the economy as a whole.

No particular virtue attaches to a person who happens to be employed in an occupation that is responsive to technology. And there is no case, in equity at least, for rewarding each type of worker according to increases in output per man hour that the advance of technology (or the improvement in managerial efficiency) make possible in the job he is doing. We do not want to broach this area of controversy just now, however.* All the reader is asked to bear in mind is that if output per man hour increases by five per cent per annum on the average in the industrial sector, national output increases by less – in our 'fifty-fifty economy', by only $2\frac{1}{2}$ per cent per annum. If workers in the industrial sector alone increased their money earnings by five per cent when the average increase in their productivity was five per cent, then the value of the additional output in the industrial sector would equal the additional money income and there would be no excess overall demand. Unit costs would remain the same and so would prices. But if the *services* sector

*Though politically unfashionable at present, it would seem far more equitable that the community as a whole should benefit from technological advances that take place in any sector. This would require money wages and salaries everywhere to be held constant over time. Increased productivity in any industry lowers the wage-costs and, therefore, the prices there. Real incomes therefore rise uniformly over the whole economy as prices fall relative to money earnings.

also claimed a five per cent increase in their money earnings, there certainly would be excess demand. Indeed, in this case if they got any increase at all in their money incomes, there would be excess overall demand. If all wanted the same increase in money income, they would have to be guided by the increase in productivity over the whole economy (services and industry together), which is $2\frac{1}{2}$ per cent. Only thus could inflation be avoided.

Now all this is straightforward arithmetic. We have yet to bring in economics. Let us then turn to the current trend of affairs in this country, in which wage concessions provide people with money earnings that exceed the rise in output as a whole, so that prices are tending upward. A 'spontaneous' addition to productivity could, of course, raise the addition to output so as to make it exactly equal to the additional money earnings handed out in the annual wage round: a sufficient increase in productivity would indeed prevent wages 'pushing up' prices. But how does one generate a 'spontaneous' addition to productivity? One can, of course, adopt measures which are intended to raise productivity. But these measures, even if they are successful in raising productivity, must be examined for the effects they have on wage demands, or on prices. For these effects may well defeat the objective of stabilizing prices.

II

Before asking what might happen to the price level by measures taken to increase productitivity, it will be useful for our understanding of these matters to ask a preliminary question: if we suppose for the moment that the annual rate of growth cannot by any means be increased above $2\frac{1}{2}$ per cent is there any policy which would hold annual wage increases to a figure no greater than $2\frac{1}{2}$ per cent? Of course the government could, as it has done in the past, attempt to 'freeze' all incomes. But if this is not an acceptable long-term solution, and if ministerial exhortations continue to prove ineffectual, is there any economie knowledge the government may avail itself of in the endeavour to limit the annual wage increase to about $2\frac{1}{2}$ per cent?

225

Twenty-one Popular Economic Fallacies

Some economists believe that the answer is a tentative yes. It is, for instance, alleged that there is a connection between the annual percentage (money) wage rise and the overall level of employment. The numerical connection may change over time, and it may become stronger or weaker. But the relationship is believed to be distinctly positive: i.e. the higher the level of total employment, the greater the annual rise in money wages. If about 5½ per cent of the employable labour force remained unemployed for a long time there would be, according to this theory, no tendency for wages to move upward. If, however, unemployment were as low as one per cent (virtually full employment, or even 'over-full' employment since there are almost certain to be more vacancies available than there are people seeking work), annual money wages may rise by six per cent or more.

A dictator could always consult the appropriate chart and choose that level of employment, say ninety-seven per cent, at which money wages (closely followed by money earnings in the rest of the economy) climb at a rate no greater than 2½ per cent per annum. With an annual overall increase in productivity of 2½ per cent prices will not rise. For the extra money income* is just equal to the value of the extra output.

A not dissimilar theory holds that price stability itself could be ensured if there were a sufficient margin of unused productive capacity in the economy. More specifically, prices would be stable, apparently irrespective of the annual rise in productivity, if employment did not rise above ninety-eight per cent.

Two difficulties may arise in trying to base a policy of price stability on either of these theories. First, we have not yet reached the degree of competence in economic controls at which

---

* We suppose that the extra *expenditure* is exactly equal to extra money income. If not, if say only three-quarters of the extra income is spent, there would be a deficiency of overall demand, and prices would tend to fall. If unchanged prices were the goal of policy, we could choose a level of employment a little higher than ninety-seven per cent, and wages therefore rising annually by somewhat more than 2½ per cent (in fact by 2½ per cent *times* 4/3, or 3⅓ per cent), so that the annual increase of overall *expenditure* would be exactly 2½ per cent, and equal to the overall increase in productivity.

governments could be confident of maintaining employment at a steady figure of ninety-seven or ninety-eight per cent, or whatever the required figure is, year in and year out. Secondly, even if the government could control the overall employment figure at the desired level, this level might be too low to be politically acceptable. If, for example, the electorate would put out of office a government that permitted two per cent or more unemployment, some degree of inflation would, with these theories, appear to be unavoidable in the absence of price controls.*

There is, however, a third theory to the effect that even if the level of employment is so high as to cause too high a rise in money wages with the result that prices start to move upwards, the government can effectively intervene without lowering the level of employment and without imposing direct controls on prices. It can pursue 'a more vigorous monetary policy'. After all, the government has ultimate control of the money supply. If, therefore, instead of allowing money to be increased to 'meet the needs of industry' at any price-level that would result from higher money wages, it decided to hold the money supply unchanged, prices could not rise. It may be argued that industry as a whole may respond by making more intensive use of the money it already had – what is sometimes referred to as an increase in the 'velocity of circulation' of money – and so defeat the government's intentions. But if the government went further and actually reduced the supply of money (by selling bonds to the public, and to the banks, in exchange for their bank balances) business firms would begin to find it harder to borrow additional money to pay their employees. The firms may be willing enough to meet the demands of union leaders (cost-push), or to bid up wages in the market (demand-pull), but unless the banks are ready to finance these extra payments they will be quite unable to

*The prospect of two per cent unemployment or more over the year would be less intolerable if unemployment benefits were much higher than they are at present, say about two-thirds of the customary earnings of the newly unemployed workers. However, any rise in unemployment pay is likely to change the relationship between the annual wage claim and the level of employment.

do so. The one argument against this proposal is that a vigorous money policy of this sort *might* suddenly depress the level of employment – 'send the economy into a tailspin' is the common phrase. No one can say that this is impossible. But as yet no generally acceptable evidence either way has been produced.

These various theories all suggest ways of stabilizing prices other than by an increase in the annual rate of productivity. Excess aggregate demand, and therefore inflation, can be reduced to zero either by operating as directly as possible on the level of employment (say by increasing taxes or reducing government expenditure, or both), or else by operating directly to reduce the total supply of money in the economy (so lowering the prices of bonds and reducing the value of the public's assets). None of these theories, however, would exclude faster economic growth as a way of stabilizing prices. Indeed, on the first theory, we could set the level of employment as high as we like, say ninety-nine per cent. Money wages may then rise annually by six per cent. But if we could increase annual productivity by about six per cent also, we should still have price stability. Before going any further, therefore, it seems pertinent to ask whether we are indeed able to increase the pace of economic growth. Clearly, the government's favourite policy of imploring the nation to do so has not been a rousing success.

III

But once we turn to measures calculated to stimulate economic growth it is only to enable us to confess that economists know very little about this subject. Phenomenal rates of growth over a period of years have been registered by many countries, by countries recovering from the ravages of war, by Continental countries still having technologically retarded sectors (including farming), and by economically immature countries. A poorer country, provided it is able to borrow money abroad or squeeze enough savings from its citizens, has an opportunity of catching up quickly by importing the advanced technology and skills of the richer countries. There may be some difficulties in adapting some modern techniques to the more backward areas of such a country, but whatever techniques are employed they are largely a free gift, the end product of continuous technological evolution. Their costs, in terms of prolonged research, experimentation, and incidental costly mistakes, have already been borne by the economically advanced countries. A mature economy, such as that of the United States, on the other hand, can continue to advance only by exerting continuous pressure along the frontier of technology – by investing large sums in the attempts to discover both new products and more efficient methods of production.

In such mature economies, it is therefore not so much the net savings of people, or the net accumulation of capital *per se* over time, that contributes to growth, but the process of technological innovation – a process which is promoted by the willingness of businessmen, or governments, to take risks in investing in and introducing new technology.

The large sums invested in industrial research may ensure that the actual flow in innovations is fairly steady over time in some sense. But the willingness of businessmen to invest money in adopting some of the more daring innovations is alleged to be subject, in large measure, to the climate of the economy. The greater the state of business confidence about the future the more likely are businessmen to take risks in trying out new methods and products. A buoyant atmosphere is associated with expanding markets, if not in the expected growth in the number of customers then in the growth of their real incomes. A buoyant atmosphere is also connected with expectations of rising prices over time.

There are, as one might expect, contrary arguments to the effect that industry becomes more competitive during a recession. During hard times, it is alleged, competition becomes keener, the inefficient managers are weeded out, and there is pressure to keep down costs and to adopt cost-reducing innovations. One can legitimately argue that at a lower level of employment the rate of growth is faster for the economy as a whole.

All this is rather speculative, as the facts do not point clearly

in either direction. Without, then, being sure of what sort of
measures, and what sort of economic climate, are most likely to
encourage economic growth, we must turn finally to the question
of whether faster economic growth, however it occurs, has the
incidental effect of stabilizing prices.

If we look at the crude facts and compare countries having
different growth rates, or compare different periods of growth in
the same country, we find no clear association between growth
and price-stability – either for high growth rates and stable
prices or for the reverse, low growth rates and stable prices.
Germany, for instance, had a higher average productivity over
the period 1950–1964 than France – about $6\frac{1}{2}$ per cent per annum
compared with about $4\frac{1}{2}$ per cent per annum. But Germany's
average annual rate of inflation was $2\frac{1}{4}$ per cent, or about half
that experienced in France over the same period. Such comparisons would seem to support the contention that faster rates of
productivity promote price stability. But now let us turn to the
Japanese experience. There was plenty of technological leeway
to be made up in that country. Its extraordinary rate of economic
growth, averaging, over the 1950–1964 period, about $9\frac{1}{2}$ per cent
per annum is therefore not too mysterious. In contrast, Britain's
growth performance was one of the lowest among the advanced
industrial nations, about $2\frac{1}{4}$ per cent per annum on the average
over the period in question.* Both countries, incidentally,
suffered from 'stop-go' policies, although the fluctuations in
income and employment were more marked in Japan. But, in
contrast to the comparison between France and Germany,
inflation in this comparison was greater in the faster growing
economy. The rate of price increase in Japan averaged close to
6 per cent per annum over the period compared with about
$4\frac{1}{2}$ per cent for Britain. The crude evidence is not such as to
warrant any provisional inference that high productivity can
be depended upon to combat inflation.

*Yet this $2\frac{1}{4}$ per cent per annum was well above the average rate of
growth experienced in Britain between 1900 and 1950, a period over which
prices in Britain rose at a much slower rate than they did in the post-war
period.

20 Economic Growth Removes Poverty

'Economic growth is necessary to remove poverty.'

Growthmen, not averse to a little moral support for their advocacy of 'faster and yet faster', are prone to harp on the theme of growth-created opportunities which lie ahead: more medical research, better hospitals, more adult education, larger parks, and more comfortable prisons. Economic growth, we are also led to believe, makes charity obsolete and is the precondition of expanding welfare services.

We may concede that economic growth is almost synonymous with greater productive power. We may further concede that the faster is economic growth the more of these collective social goods might be produced over the future without any reduction of the existing kinds of goods.* But will they? And do we need to wait for more economic growth before we can have more of these things?

We shall be content here to argue that economic growth is neither necessary nor sufficient for the removal of poverty, though the arguments can be extended to other social desiderata.

I

Poverty is obviously a relative state of affairs with respect to both time and place. In Britain today over two million people are eligible to receive supplementary benefits from the National Assistance Board. These people may be thought of as comprising

---

* I say 'might' in order to remind the reader that although all man-made goods do or should enter the national product, the man-made 'bads' or adverse 'spillover effects' that are incidental to the productive process do not. (See Chapter 21.) If they could be included we should discover whether the value of extra goods was enough to offset the value of the extra 'bads'. For argument's sake, however, we shall assume that there is *net* growth in this sense.

the 'hard core' poverty group. A single man or woman with weekly cash receivings below £4 6s. 0d. (excluding rent allowance) may apply for cash benefits that will make up weekly cash receipts to that figure. For a married couple the figure is £7 1s. 0d. (excluding rent allowance).* In Britain today, where average earnings per worker are a little over £20 a week, and much more than that for the average family, the plight of these two million warrants sympathy. In so rich a country as Britain their relative poverty is degrading. Yet a working-class couple in India having the equivalent of £7 a week to dispose of would think itself favoured by providence. There, average earnings work out at roughly 25s. a week. And *per capita* income (national income divided by total population) is something like 10s. a week.

Again, although average earnings in Britain are a little over £20 a week, or £1,000 a year, American economists draw the poverty line in the United States at £1,400, or more, for a four-person family.† A great number of British families, believing themselves to be in fairly comfortable circumstances, might feel a bit put out to discover that, by American standards, they would be classified among the deserving poor.

But however the poor are defined there is every prospect that, as the New Testament affirms, they will always be with us. If real national income rises by, say, ten per cent over a period, and everyone enjoys a rise of ten per cent, including the poor, then the poor remain in exactly the same position *relative* to the rest of the population. But it happens that those comprising the hard core poverty group – a large proportion of whom are

*An additional allowance of between 30s. and 40s. for rent is made by the Board, with the result that many who depend wholly, or almost wholly, on their pensions – minimum £4 10s. 0d. for a single person, £7 6s. 0d. for a married couple – may also be receiving assistance from the Board.

†The poverty line was drawn by some writers at $3,000 in 1959, which is worth about $4,000 today (1968) or, *at the present exchange rate*, about £1,700. Other writers have drawn it at $2,600 in 1959, and $3,000 in 1963 – or about $3,500 at 1968 prices. At the present exchange rate this is about £1,400. A more realistic rate of conversion would reduce the pound equivalent of the American figures by about a quarter. But even so, their poverty line would be far above that in Britain.

pensioners, or too old or too incapacitated to work – do not share directly in the growing 'real' income of the community. Whatever increase in money income they can hope to receive will depend upon what the government is prepared to grant them, either as an increase in pension rights or as supplementary benefits. Worse still, their 'real' standards are likely to fall for long periods over which prices are rising at anything between three to six per cent per annum while their money pensions (and supplementary benefits) remain unchanged.

II

It should be obvious, however, that even if economic growth did serve to reduce poverty over time, it is not *necessary*. Of course, if we refuse to reduce all other items of expenditure, public and private; if we refuse to reduce expenditure on defence research, investment and consumption; if we refuse to tax a large number of luxury and semi-luxury goods, then we cannot help the poor more than we are doing. The politicians may argue that it is 'politically unfeasible' which phrase, if taken seriously, means simply that the electorate does not wish to transfer expenditure away from any other goods in order to give more to the poor. If this is a fact (which I doubt) there is no more to be said except to emphasize that the decision not to give more aid to the poor today is a purely political decision: there is nothing of 'economic necessity' about it.

As things stand, a sum equal to £500 million – hardly more than half the average annual increase of our real national income – would enable us to double the annual expenditure on the poor in this hard core category. It would make their life tolerable, if not comfortable. A twenty per cent tax on a post-tax expenditure of £2,500 million of luxury and semi-luxury goods would also effect the desired transfer. So would a reduction of our defence budget by about a quarter. Any of these measures, or a combination of them, are economically feasible. The country would continue to survive, and no great hardship would be inflicted on any section of the public.

A far simpler alternative, however, and one which should have more immediate appeal, would involve no more than a re-allocation of some part of our annual public expenditure on welfare services, currently running at the rate of about £7,000 million. The prevailing principle of universality of benefits presents every retired earner with a state pension though, obviously, not each of them needs a state pension. In fact, about every other couple receiving a state pension has (according to the 1966 Pension Survey) an income of £10 a week or more. The state, also, is prepared to finance every child's schooling. Yet a considerable proportion of the families whose children's schooling is so financed would be quite able and willing, if necessary, to pay the full cost of their children's school education. Again the state provides us all with a free health service notwithstanding that the majority of the families in this country could well afford to pay for the medical care it requires (and that all but a very small proportion of the population could afford to pay the full prescription charges). What is more, the current demand on the resources of the health service by the population as a whole is unnecessarily large – which is not surprising. One does not need a training in economics to realize that people will want more of a commodity or service that is provided free than if, instead, they are charged the full cost of the resources required to provide it. That people 'over-use' the health service is the most common complaint of the doctors. This observation does not, however, exclude an economic argument for subsidizing particular medical services to most people, or even of providing all medical service free to particular groups of people.* But no economic case has been established for providing all medical care free to everyone, rich and poor alike.

What then prevents the state from employing the selectivity principle in the distribution of the welfare services? In this instance, what prevents the state from redirecting a portion of the vast resources it uses in providing universal benefits away from those whose need of state aid is small in order to increase the scale of benefits for the group forming the hard core of

* See Chapter 6.

poverty? The answer, strangely enough, is the opposition of many socialists and trade unionists. In accordance with the universalist principle there are socialists who insist on providing the rich with what are to them trifling cash benefits in order that the really poor need not feel ashamed of accepting them also. In addition, there are the older members of the work force for whom the so-called Means Test cannot but evoke bitter memories of the inter-war period. Admittedly the Means Test was an unpleasant procedure by current standards of administration. But discrimination in the provision of benefits, either in money or kind, is transparently impossible without some means of ascertaining need. The resources are at hand and, in a rational community, the only issue would be that of devising a simpler, speedier, and more acceptable method of collecting the minimum information necessary to ensure that increased benefits, which can be made available in this way, are received by those most in need of them.

The facts and the arguments are familiar enough to economists who, in this instance, have often set out the alternative choices facing the community with commendable clarity.* But it is an uphill struggle. Such is the power of pride and prejudice in the modern world that the barrier to the most immediate and effective method of helping the needy to a decent standard of living – in effect wiping out the really degrading poverty that is totally unnecessary in a country as wealthy as Britain – is held in place by idealistic socialists and trade unionists, the very group that should be in the forefront of any movement to bring about a redistribution of the national output in favour of the poor and the incapacitated.

III

Granted that economic growth is not necessary, is it sufficient? In other words, in the absence of all state-sponsored measures

*A recent and excellent discussion of the issues will be found in the December 1967 issue of *Encounter* by Arthur Seldon of the Institute of Economic Affairs.

for alleviating poverty, would economic growth alone over time bring about a diminution of poverty? Two reasons suggest that economic growth alone will not suffice.

First, as we have seen, poverty, even hard core poverty, is a relative term: even if the poor share in the growing 'real' wealth no less than the rest of the community, they would still qualify as poor. Thus, even if we succeed in realizing the highest aspirations of our growthmen, and eventually 'catch up with the Americans', we should, like them, be contributing larger absolute sums towards the subsistence of the 'new' poor who would, of course, in 'real' terms, be better off than the poor are today – while still being as poor as before compared with the rest of the population. Indeed, even though their relative material position will remain unchanged, the new poor may somehow feel worse off in a more affluent society. Arnold Toynbee has observed that America is the worst country in the world to be poor in.

Secondly, as already indicated, a large proportion of the very poor do not in fact share in the growing 'real' wealth simply because many are unemployable or very nearly so. Either they suffer from some physical or mental handicap or they are just too old to work under modern conditions. Without help from relations, and in the absence of state relief or private charities, they would simply expire from hunger and exposure.

Even if we turn our sights towards the lowest income-earning groups there is no clear evidence to suggest that the process of economic growth particularly favours them. On the contrary, recent American writing suggests that the groups which offer the greatest opportunities for the elimination of poverty – families below some arbitrarily drawn poverty line – appear, to some extent, to be isolated from economic growth. Indeed, there are some who believe that the limited decline of absolute poverty in the United States which can be attributed to economic growth may become smaller in the future.* This would mean that even if

---

*There is not yet complete agreement among economists on the facts. L. Galloway (*American Economic Review*, March 1965) concluded that economic growth could play a prominent role over time in reducing (absolute) poverty. His results, however, have been the subject of attack

economic growth alone and unaided could eliminate domestic poverty in an absolute sense, though not in a relative sense, it would take many years to accomplish. We conclude, tentatively, that only direct government action, using the method of selective benefits, can make an immediate impact on the problem of hard core poverty, and can reduce it in both an absolute and a relative sense.

IV

While we are on the subject we may as well glance briefly at another prize piece of growth-inspired humbug – the argument that only faster economic growth will enable us to fulfil our obligations to the so-called underdeveloped regions of the world – meaning the poorer countries of Asia, Africa and South America which contain nearly two-thirds of the world's population. Now if, in response to a moral challenge, the richer countries of the West agreed to transform themselves into an arsenal for the provision of food, clothing, medicines and machinery to the world's underprivileged multitudes, the question might arise: what difference to their standards of living could we make over what given period of time? (Incidentally, however we went about finding an answer, it would always depend on the success achieved in restricting the growth of their populations.)

But such a question does not arise simply because, notwithstanding a good deal of oratory on the subject at international gatherings, the actual scale of such aid is unimpressive, and more suggestive of 'conscience money' (to use Professor Bauer's words) than of deep concern. The annual aid given to poor countries by the largest donor, the United States – a country

by H. Aaron (*American Economic Review*, December 1967) whose analysis reveals that Galloway's results are unreliable, and that the *aggregate* poverty statistics he employs are inherently incapable of providing evidence for or against the thesis that poverty will disappear over time as a result of economic growth alone. Moreover, Aaron shows that among some groups, such as white farm households, poverty is sensitive to economic growth, while among other groups, non-farm groups, non-white groups, and female-headed families, poverty is barely affected by economic growth.

fearful of excess capacity in its basic and manufacturing industries, and prone always to overproduction in its foodstuffs – amounts to well under one per cent of its gross national product.*
With steady economic growth at an average of three per cent per annum, which is optimistic, more than two decades would be needed to double this trickle of aid to the poorer countries.

* Both the limited ability of these poor countries to absorb economic aid, and the fear of a balance-of-payments problem, are sometimes invoked to explain the glaring discrepancy between words and deeds. Neither carries conviction.

There may indeed be difficulties in persuading indigenous populations to use Western techniques. And it may be costly to train them to operate modern machinery. But there should be no difficulty in meeting the immediate needs of people for foodstuffs, clothing, books, medical supplies, pesticides, contraceptives and farm implements in order to alleviate physical and mental distress.

As for the balance-of-payments problem, if the United States guaranteed to provide, say, ten per cent of its annual income to India, that country would be more than glad to accept it annually as a 'tied' gift – that is, subject to the condition that the dollars received were spent entirely in the United States.

21 Economic Growth Enriches Society

'Economic growth necessarily enriches society.

This belief is held by some to be self-evident, provided economic growth is the result not of mere population increase but rather of a rise in real income *per capita*. If we suppose this to be the case it would seem that the grounds for belief rest on a sequence of causal statements:

(*a*) Economic growth causes more goods to be available for most people.

(*b*) An increase of the amount of goods available to a person implies an extension in his area of choice.

(*c*) An extension of the area of his choice must cause an increase in his welfare, i.e. it 'enriches' his life.

Ergo, per capita economic growth enriches society. However, as we shall show below, each of these three statements – by which a rise in *per capita* 'real' income over time is linked to an increase in welfare – is untenable. Before considering each in turn, however, let us be clear about the meaning of 'an extension of the area of choice'. This extension is deemed to take place if a person's income buys a selection of goods hitherto unattainable. If, for instance, nothing changes over the years except that the prices of carrots and silk ties fall steadily, a person's unchanged money income enables him to buy exactly the same amounts of all other goods along with more carrots and silk ties. If he never buys carrots or silk ties he will not benefit from their fall in price. He will continue to buy exactly the same collection of goods as before. In that case he cannot be supposed to be better off; though even here we might talk of a *potential* expansion of choice even if it is not made effective.

If, on the other hand, he does avail himself of the lower prices

239

of carrots and silk ties to buy a different collection of goods (hitherto unavailable to him), the extension of the area of his choice is clearly manifest. In that case, since he could have continued to buy the old collection of goods, but chooses instead to buy a new collection (which was previously unavailable) one must suppose he prefers the new to the old. And that also, therefore, he is better off with the new collection than with the old. But we are 'jumping the gun' with this last inference that he is better off, as indeed the economist is prone to do. We shall ignore it then, and remain satisfied with the explanation of what is meant, in an economic context, by 'an extension of the area of choice'.

Let us now examine, in turn, each of the above three statements in the light of the world around us.

I

(a) We start with a criticism of the view that economic growth results in most people having more goods. It is, of course, acceptable to define economic growth as a rise in *per capita* productive power. So defined, it is clear that economic growth at least *allows* of an increase in goods, so that every one *could* have more goods than before. This is in fact the very limited sense in which the statement is valid: in a strictly potential sense. For in the process of economic growth the actual kinds of goods being produced are continuously changing. Some of today's collection of goods being produced were not previously seen in the shops; they may be called novelties. Others are like the old goods, but are more efficient or of better quality or design. Now if these new goods appear on the market while the old goods are still available, there is no question but that, by definition, a greater variety of goods is available. And if most people's incomes *enable* them to buy as much or more of the old goods (without working any harder) plus the opportunity of buying some entirely new goods, then there is an acceptable sense to the statement that economic growth has made more goods available for most people. But – and this is important – if he can no longer buy the old selection of goods, if they are withdrawn from the market or if their prices have become too high, the statement does not hold.

If, therefore, in the process of economic growth, brands and models and types of goods are continually being withdrawn and replaced by others, as does occur in the real world, we cannot legitimately talk of *more* goods being available to a person – at least not without some satisfactory method of equating new goods with old. And this, as it happens, cannot be done unless they exist side by side for the consumer to choose from.

II

(b) However, even if no goods were ever withdrawn from the market at the discretion of manufacturers, but all the old goods continued to appear at the same or lower prices at the same time as new goods were offered to the public, we could not infer that a person whose income was now able to buy more of the old goods* enjoyed an expansion of the range of choices confronting him. Not unless we are sure also that no 'bads' are being simultaneously introduced by the growth processes. Let me explain: in so far as I now have the *option* of flying to Bermuda at a known price whereas formerly I could only go by ship, the addition of this new option surely constitutes at least a potential extension in the range of choices facing me. But if a 'bad' is thrown in without consulting me, in the form of continual disturbance from aircraft noise, there is also a subtraction from my choice. The 'bad' inflicted can reasonably be regarded as a good – peace and quiet – that is arbitrarily taken from me. And if so, there is no longer a net expansion in the choices facing me. If, of course, I were fully compensated for the noise I was suffered to bear, so that I was equally content with having the noise and the compensation together as I was in the absence of the noise, then indeed the new option of flying to Bermuda adds something net to the choices facing me. But in the absence of full compensation to offset the 'bad', it is far from impossible that I should prefer the pre-exist-

* It makes no difference to the argument whether in fact he does buy more of the old goods or whether instead he buys fewer of them along with some of the new goods.

ing situation, one in which I had my peace and quiet without the opportunity for air travel, even if it were free.

If such a choice were given to me, I might well indicate my preference by choosing the no-air-travel situation. But within the present legal framework such a choice is not offered me. The financial columns may point to the increased opportunities for people. The index of 'real' national income may rise. The economist may indicate that my own 'real' income has risen. But I may be quite sure that I am worse off, because one of the things I value most (and which was once free) is not to be had at any price – or to be had only at a price I cannot afford.

This is only one example of a large number of 'bads' – or adverse 'spillover effects' as they are referred to by economists – that are being thrown up in increasing amounts in the process of economic growth. There is, among other interesting by-products of economic activity, a continuing growth of smog and air pollution; of effluent in rivers, lakes and seas; of noise from ground traffic, air traffic, lawn mowers and diesel saws; of congestion in the towns and cities, of visual disturbance and uglification; of radioactive poisoning from nuclear fission and from the disposal of the waste products of atomic energy plants, all having far-reaching ecological effects on animal and plant life. Such consequences constitute a proliferation of 'bads', or an arbitrary deprivation of goods once enjoyed, which results from the process of making available to the consumer more man-made goods, not many of which are as valuable to the good life as manufacturers would like to persuade us. If these 'bads', or negative goods, were properly evaluated and entered annually into the estimates of 'real' national income it might well disclose a prolonged decline of economic growth over the years.*

* Clearly the effect such 'bads' would have on a national income index that is revised to include them would depend on the value of the loss attributed to the 'bads'. The value attached to them should in principle be equal to the *minimal* compensation necessary to induce all people affected to accept them. In some cases, however, it may cost less to use technical means to eliminate completely the 'bad' in question. For example, it may be cheaper for the manufacturer to install smokeless chimneys than to compensate people for the damages sustained.

III

There are yet other arbitrary changes accompanying economic growth which may be good, bad or indifferent, but which nonetheless do not belong to the range of choices over which a person has control. Economic growth, we need hardly remind ourselves, is largely the result of technological changes. Even if a person holds on to the same job, he is obliged over time to change his methods of work if he is to continue in that employment. He might like, as he grows older, to continue in the same old way at the same old pay, and in a community, nay, in a world, that remains familiar to him. But his wishes in this respect will not decide the issue – not for long at any rate, even though his trade union supports him. Sooner or later productivity considerations will override the occupational preference of the workers. True, if he continues in employment despite technological change he will have a choice of more market goods than before. But whether he would prefer to remain with the previous choice of market goods and work in the old way, will not be known to us. He may rationally prefer the old situation and, therefore, be unambiguously worse off in the new situation – notwithstanding which all the indices will point to a rise in his 'real' income.

IV

(c) We turn now to the final link, connecting economic growth with welfare. Even if there were a continuous expansion of choice in the most acceptable sense – that is, all goods and no 'bads', or clear evidence of a preponderance of goods over bads – there is no assurance that a person gains increased satisfaction therefrom for at least five reasons:

(i) Owing to the lack of appropriate legislation, and to the lack of a more efficient information service for consumers, the consumer has little knowledge of the ingredients and chemicals that enter into the foodstuffs he buys. Even if he were given a list of them, he would be unlikely to have any understanding of their long-run effects on his health. To some extent this is due to the fact that the medical profession is uncertain, or currently

243

divided about the long-term effects of certain common chemicals used in manufactured foodstuffs. Similarly with drugs. Scores of new drugs and preparations appear each year on the market, all supposedly tested. Yet, as we are discovering, drugs that yesterday were regarded as having no harmful side-effects may be discovered to be a prime cause of one or a number of fatal diseases. The buyer may choose freely foodstuffs or drugs hitherto unavailable to him, but he may be doing himself physical harm. He may regret the choices he makes. Though anticipating an increase in his welfare he may end up with an increase in 'illfare'.

(*ii*) Furthermore, the proliferation of variety itself does not necessarily provide increased welfare. Confining ourselves to hardware, where the effects on our physical health at least appear negligible, the growth in designs and models of electric goods is enough to baffle the expert. The ordinary consumer, faced with eighty-nine different kinds of transistor, thirty-seven different models of washing machine, 123 different models of electric fire, forty-four different vacuum cleaners, to say nothing of continual additions to and subtractions from the existing variety on the market, is not known to complain of lack of variety in this respect. Despite all the existing consumer research this sort of variety is too much for him. It becomes a liability, a cost. It uses up time and causes more anxiety than satisfaction. His welfare would be more likely to increase if the variety were smaller, and the differences between models more clearly differentiated. But this alternative choice of having a smaller and more clearly differentiated range of products is not presented to him by the market.

(*iii*) So far we have assumed his tastes or preferences to remain unchanged. Once they do change over time, there is no (objective) way of determining whether he is better or worse off. Even if his income commands more of all goods, he can become less satisfied than before if, for any reason, his capacity to enjoy goods is diminishing.

This is not far-fetched. Modern advertising, taken as a whole, conspires first to make men feel that the things that matter to them are the material things of life: the goods and services and opportunities provided by the economy. Second, it conspires to make men dissatisfied with what they have – so goading them into efforts to increase their 'real' earnings so as to acquire more of the stuff produced by modern industry. It is far from impossible, then, that although the tide of consumer goods and services rises steadily over time for nearly every person in the Western world, dissatisfaction with his lot grows faster yet.

(*iv*) Familiarity with what is known to economists as 'the relative income hypothesis' does, in any case, suggest that a man's satisfaction – at least in the wealthier countries, such as Britain – does not depend so much upon his 'real' wealth in the absolute sense measured by the index of real income, but upon his position in the income structure. If a man's salary were increased by ten per cent without any change in the income of his associates, he would probably feel gratified. If national income increased over three years or so by ten per cent, and every person shared equally in the increase, few would feel much satisfaction. Indeed, any whose incomes increased by less, say by only five per cent, would be likely to feel worse off than they did in the previous situation, that in which indeed their position in the income-hierarchy was better.

This hypothesis alone, for which there is ample evidence, is enough to make one sceptical of any connection between real national product and social welfare.

(*v*) Finally, there are consequences arising from the preconditions and processes of economic growth itself that bear strongly on human welfare. They can be decisive, but they are not measurable. Most important of these is the growing anonymity of life as technology finds ever more efficient ways of producing goods and services. For, to a large extent, technological efficiency involves substituting remote controls for direct human services, and making people less dependent on communication with others for their needs and entertainment. Those old-fashioned enough to believe that the chief sources of gratification are to be found in intimate personal relationships and the sense of belonging to a community cannot view the advance of an all-embracing technology without misgivings.